Thomas K. [from old catalog] Serrano

Between Two Fires

Thomas K. [from old catalog] Serrano

Between Two Fires

ISBN/EAN: 9783337054434

Printed in Europe, USA, Canada, Australia, Japan

Cover: Foto ©Thomas Meinert / pixelio.de

More available books at **www.hansebooks.com**

A COMEDY DRAMA

IN THREE ACTS

BY

THOMAS K SERRANO

PRINTED FROM THE AUTHOR'S MANUSCRIPT WITH THE CAST OF THE CHAR-
ACTERS SYNOPSIS OF INCIDENTS TIME OF REPRESENTATION COSTUMES
SCENE AND PROPERTY PLOTS DIAGRAMS OF THE STAGE SET-
TINGS SIDES OF ENTRANCE AND EXIT RELATIVE POSI-
TIONS OF THE PERFORMERS EXPLANATION OF
THE STAGE DIRECTIONS TABLEAUX ETC
AND ALL OF THE STAGE BUSINESS

NEW YORK
HAROLD ROORBACH, PUBLISHER
9 MURRAY STREET

BETWEEN TWO FIRES.

CAST OF CHARACTERS.

COLONEL LUNDY, - - A man with an eventful history.
JEROME EDDY, - A gentleman of means, residing at Fort Lee.
ROBERT, - - - { His adopted son, a youth who stands "Between two Fires."
PATRICK GREENVILLE, { Lawyers by profession and adventurers by
FRANÇOIS BULLAY, { nature.
JOSÉ MASSINI, - - - - - - An adventurer.
PRIVATE O'ROURKE, { An Irishman who does not think he descended from the Kings of Ireland.
FRITZ, - - - - Whose prudence equals his gallantry.
LOUISA DE MORI, - A Creole lady sojourning at the north.
ROWENA, - - - - - - - - Her daughter.
MRS. JULIET GREENVILLE, A non-believer in judicial separation.
OFFICERS, SOLDIERS, ETC.

NOTE.—The characters of EDDY and MASSINI can be doubled without inconvenience.

TIME OF REPRESENTATION—TWO HOURS AND A HALF.

SYNOPSIS OF INCIDENTS.

ACT I. At Fort Lee, on the Hudson. News from the war. The meeting. The colonel's strange romance. Departing for the war. The intrusted packet. An honest man. A last request. Bitter hatred. The dawn of love. A Northerner's sympathy for the South. Is he a traitor? Held in trust. La Creole gold mine for sale. Financial agents. A brother's wrong. An order to cross the enemy's lines. Fortune's fool. Love's penalty. Man's independence. Strange disclosures. Discarded. A shadowed life. Beggared in pocket and bankrupt in love. His last chance. The refusal. Turned from home. Alone, without a name. Off to the war.

ACT II. On the battlefield. An Irishman's philosophy. Unconscious of danger. Spies in the camp. The insult. Risen from the ranks. The colonel's prejudice. Letters from home. The plot to ruin. A token of love. True to him. The plotters at work. Breaking the seals. The meeting of husband and wife. A forlorn hope. Doomed as a spy. A struggle for lost honor. A soldier's death.

ACT III. Before Richmond. The home of Mrs. De Mori. The two documents. A little misunderstanding. A deserted wife. The truth revealed. Brought to light. Mother and child. Rowena's sacrifice. The American Eagle spreads his wings. The spider's web. True to himself. The reconciliation. A long divided home reunited. The close of the war.

COSTUMES.

LUNDY. *Act I:* Dark frock coat, buttoned up close; light trowsers; gloves; silk hat; cane. *Acts II and III:* Uniform of a colonel, U. S. A.

EDDY. Dark trowsers and vest; dressing-gown and slippers.

ROBERT. *Act I:* Dark cutaway coat, with waistcoat; light trowsers; derby hat; patent leather shoes. *Act II:* Uniform of a sergeant, U. S. A. *Act III:* Officer's uniform, U. S. A.

GREENVILLE and BULLAY. Business suits; derby hats. Bullay has a seal attached to his watch chain.

MASSINI. Confederate private's uniform.

O'ROURKE. Uniform of a private, U. S. A.

FRITZ. *Acts I and III:* Black swallow-tail coat; black low-cut vest; black trowsers; highly starched shirt-front, turn-down collar and white necktie. *Act II:* Uniform of a private, U. S. A.

LOUISA. } *Act I:* Handsome street toilets. *Act II:* Traveling costumes. *Act III:* Plain black house dresses,
ROWENA. } with very little jewelry.

MRS. GREENVILLE. Handsome traveling dress, bonnet, gloves and parasol.

STAGE SETTINGS.

ACT I.

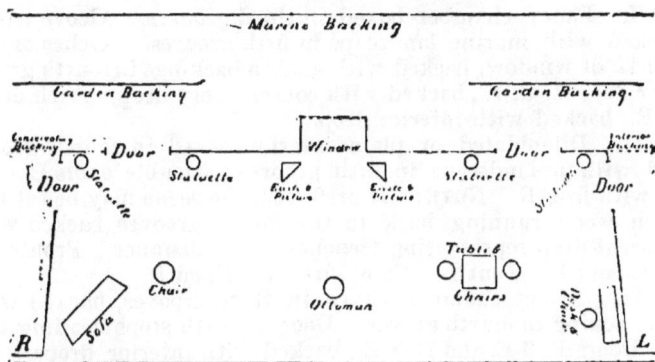

ACT II.

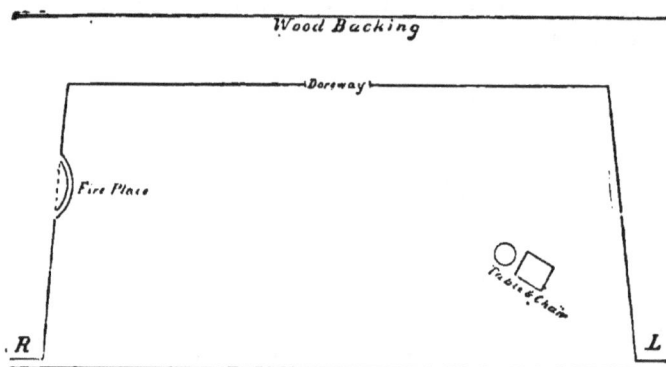

ACT III.

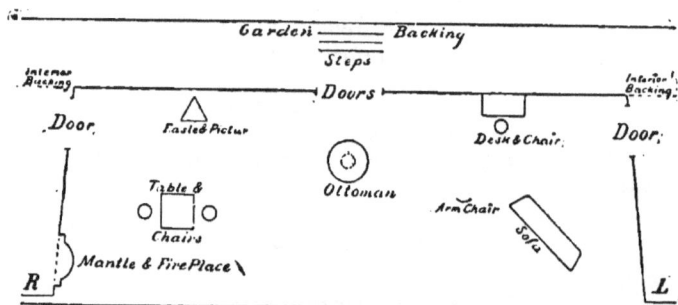

SCENE PLOT.

ACT I. Fancy chamber boxed in third grooves. Alcove window
C., backed with marine landscape in fifth grooves. Arches or doors
R. and L. of window, backed with garden backings in fourth grooves.
Arch or door R. U. E., backed with conservatory drop. Arch or door
L. U. E., backed with interior drop.

ACT II. Dilapidated or plain interior, boxed in fourth grooves,
backed with a landscape in fifth grooves. Double doors C. Fire-
place, with fire, R. NOTE: If preferred, the scene may be set thus:
an open wood running back to the fourth grooves, backed with a
transparent drop representing trenches in the distance. Profile wood
wings R. and L. Tent L. Camp-fire and tripod R.

ACT III. Fancy chamber boxed in third grooves, backed with a
garden backing in fourth groves. Door C., with steps leading down
to it. Doors R. 3 E. and L. 3 E., backed with interior drops. Fire-
place and mantel down R.

PROPERTIES.

ACT I. Handsome suit of furniture. Carpet and medallion down. Pedestals supporting statuettes, R. and L. of doors in flat. Desk, or secretary, with writing materials, down L. Easels and pictures R. and L. of window. Plants in the conservatory, R. Newspapers for FRITZ. Coin money for MRS. GREENVILLE. Bank-notes for GREENVILLE, also a cigar in case. Blank will and cigarettes for BULLAY. Packet of letters for LUNDY. Cut flowers for ROWENA. Drum and fife outside.

ACT II. Table and chair down L. Flask, packet of letters, and documents for BULLAY. Flask, pipe, packet of letters, musket and documents for O'ROURKE. Muskets and accoutrements for SOLDIERS. Bugle, drum and fife. Red fire, for fire. Bass drum to imitate the noise of cannon. Cigars and cigarettes for GREENVILLE and BULLAY. Tobacco and pipe for ROBERT. Two packets for OFFICER. Despatch for ORDERLY. Field glass and writing materials on table down L.

ACT III. Handsome suit of furniture. Carpet matting, with medallion down. Ottoman C. Oblong mirror and bric-a-brac on mantel. Table, with books and ornaments on it, and two chairs R. C. Easy chair L. C. Sofa down L. Desk or secretary up L. C. Easel, bearing a picture, up R. C. Packet of letters for BULLAY. Sealed Packet and envelope for O'ROURKE. Letter for MASSINI. Documents for GREENVILLE and MRS. DE MORI.

STAGE DIRECTIONS.

The player is supposed to be facing the audience. R. means right ; L., left ; C., centre ; R. C., right of centre ; L. C., left of centre ; D. F., door in the flat or scene running across the back of the stage; R. F., right side of the flat; L. F., left side of the flat; R. D., right door ; L. D., left door ; 1 E., first entrance ; 2 E., second entrance ; U. E., upper entrance ; 1, 2 or 3 G., first, second or third grooves ; up stage—toward the back ; down stage—toward the footlights.

R.   R. C.   C.   L. C.   L.

BETWEEN TWO FIRES.

ACT I.

Scene.—*Drawing-room in* JEROME EDDY'S *house at Fort-Lee. Time, morning. At the rise of the curtain,*—JEROME EDDY *is discovered in dressing gown and slippers, writing a letter at desk* L. H. Enter FRITZ R. U. E., *with newspapers ; he crosses* L. *to* EDDY.

Fritz. (*Approaching* EDDY.) I hopes dot I don't intrude mit you, Sir ; but dere newspapers vas come.

Eddy. (*Addressing envelope.*) Very well, Fritz ; just place them here on the desk. (FRITZ *places papers on desk and attempts to go off* L. U. E.) Stay ! (*Sealing letter.*) You'll take this letter to Colonel Lundy ; you will find him at his rooms. Wait for an answer. (*Gives letter to* FRITZ.)

Fritz. Yaah, mister Eddy ; I vill vate for un answer. (*Aside.*) Shust der man I vish to speak mit. I tinks ich better by the var den here. Dere vork is less, dere vages more.

Exit FRITZ, R. C., *at back.*

Eddy. (*Opening newspaper.*) I wonder what's the latest news of the war. (*After looking intently at paper.*) Ah ! what's this ? " The defeat experienced by the northern forces yesterday, makes it necessary to send re-enforcements immediately. Ten thousand more men needed to fill the vacancy made by the removal of the reserve troops." If affairs continue thus, I fear another slaughter like that at Bull Run will occur. Many have left their homes and families, never to return. War ! war ! thou art a curse to civilization.

Enter COL. LUNDY, R. C., *at back.*

(*Rising.*) Ah, good morning, Colonel. (*They shake hands, then advance down stage.*)

Lundy. (*Advancing down* C.) The salutation is mutual. (*Sitting on ottaman,* C.) Apropos ; while on my way thither, I encountered Fritz, your servant, and received your letter, though I

6

confess I haven't yet opened it. (*Shows letter.*) What's the news?

Eddy. (*Resuming seat previously occupied.*) I would rather you answer that question. Tell me, Colonel, is it true you have been ordered to prepare for active service?

Lundy. Yes; I start to-day—in fact within an hour. It was to inform you of this, I hastened here.

Eddy. And it was to know what truth was in the rumor, I sent you that letter. You must indeed feel very proud over your commission. Of course, it is the ambition of every soldier to win a high place, if possible, in the service.

Lundy. True; and at the head of such a brave and gallant regiment as I am about to command, there is no reason why I should not rise a grade or two higher. A better drilled or a more orderly set of men I have never seen in all my experience. Ha! ha! ha! This going to fight these rebels gives me much pleasure. I have more than a country's bitterness at heart, especially for that class known as creoles—the miserable wretches! Before I say good-bye, I wish you take charge of this packet (*Producing packet from coat pocket*); and if I fall, I want you to break the seal, read the contents, and act according to the inclosed directions.

Eddy. Why not trust its keeping to your lawyer?

Lundy. I have no use for a lawyer. Lawyers and creoles I hate.

Eddy. Your hatred for the south, especially the creoles seems to be very intense.

Lundy. It is, and no one who knew the cause would blame me. You have ever been a good and generous friend, and if you don't mind, I will tell you—though perhaps you don't care to know.

Eddy. But I do; perhaps I may be able to advise you.

Lundy. Thanks. You must know then, that after I was graduated at West Point, I went south to settle up an estate left me by a distant relative. I was not long in Nashville, before I received an entrée into the best circles of society, and, if I may so express myself, I was considered a quite good looking fellow.

Eddy. And of course much admired by the fair sex.

Lundy. Among my acquaintances was a certain government official, of high political standing, with whose sister I fell in love and who returned my affection.

· Eddy. You were fortunate.

Lundy. Was I? You may not think so when I have finished my narrative. We were both aware that her brother, my political acquaintance, would refuse his consent to our union.

Eddy. And naturally enough, you did without it.

Lundy. Yes. The marriage was secretly solemnized and we left Nashville. Here, I must tell you, the family were of French and Mexican extraction, and, in common with the nature of all creoles, possessed a revengeful and vindictive spirit. When we made our flight, we journeyed to Mexico, where I had obtained a position in the government engineer corps. For six months I was in Paradise, only to awaken one morning to find myself in the other place. The brother had discovered our whereabouts, and, with proofs strong as Holy Writ, denounced me to the Mexican authorities, as a spy in the pay of France, sent there to ascertain their military strength. I was tried, convicted, and condemned for life.

Eddy. You? an American?

Lundy. Yes. The evidence produced was of so strong a nature, that had I been a spectator at the trial, I surely would have believed the accused guilty. I will not attempt to describe to you my sufferings; but let it suffice when I tell you, had it not been that Heaven gave me a strong and robust constitution, I should not be here now to tell my story. I would long since have forgotten the terrible tortures I endured, and even forgiven the brother, but for the bitter knowledge that the wife I so dearly loved, the wife for whom I would have died a thousand times, was the archconspirator in the plot.

Eddy. Your wife? Surely you are mistaken!

Lundy. Not at all; a letter in that packet confirms the accusation beyond a doubt. Tired of her lover, regretting her marriage, as it was a barrier to her ambition, she informed her brother of her whereabouts, and accused me of having abducted her. The brother, being wrought to that state of anger where revenge becomes master of the soul, consummated his scheme—and my imprisonment followed.

Eddy. How did you obtain your freedom?

Lundy. In company with two others, I made my escape, through the aid of a deputy jailor. My two companions died on the way across the plains, just when we were in sight of the American border ; I alone crossed the Rio Grande. After some more rough travelling, I at length reached Washington.

Eddy. Where, of course, you obtained redress ?

Lundy. Where, of course, I obtained nothing of the sort. I tried hard, but in vain, for then, as now, political influence is the axis on which the wheels of justice revolve in the different departments of the Government. I at last became weary of waiting for the Secretary to take action in the affair, and allowed my grievances to sink into oblivion. I have always been under the impression that friends of the brother—certain Southern congressmen—had much to do in the retardment of an investigation into my case. Now can you wonder at my desire to enter upon the battlefield and charge into the midst of these Southern hounds, especially the creoles, and deal them out defeat and death? Ah, the very thought of what's to come fires every energy of heart and soul, and makes me feel young again! (*Laughter heard outside* R. U. E. EDDY *goes up* C. *and looks off* R.) Who's that?

Eddy. Only my son and some lady friends of his; they are coming this way.

Lundy. Ladies are undesirable creatures with me. I'm off—I'm what may be termed a woman hater.

Eddy. (*Coming down* C.) Not so bad as that, I hope. All women, you know, are not alike—but come, I see you're growing distressed. We will go into the library and have a parting glass of wine together. There we shall be free from all intrusion. Come. (*Going towards* L. U. E.)

Lundy. (*Following* EDDY.) Who are the ladies?

Eddy. Ah, I see you have a weak spot still for the fair sex. They are—ahem—a creole lady and her daughter.

Lundy. A creole! Confound it! it's bad enough to be a woman, but a cross between a cat and a tigress—well—da——

Eddy. (*Placing hand before* LUNDY'S *mouth.*) Tut—tut—she will meet your wish, if she is not blessed (*Points upwards.*) You had better let me introduce you.

Lundy. Never, sir! never! How is it you have not encouraged Robert to enlist in behalf of his country's cause?

Eddy. I have ; but I'm sorry to confess his sympathies are with the South.

Lundy. What! with the South? And you—you shelter such

a son! Why the fellow should be quartered at Fort Lafayette, not here.

Eddy. Why I am not severe on the lad, is because of my old age. You know a man of my age desires a companion; and what better companion could he have than his own son?

Lundy. True; and on that account I can be lenient with him. By the bye, how are he and Miss Trehayne getting on? I don't see them out riding so frequently of late.

Eddy. The fact is, Colonel, he has transferred his affections to this creole girl who, although the daughter of a Southern aristocrat, is no suitable helpmate through life for him. This I have told him, and, would you believe me, he has actually refused to recognise my right in the matter.

Lundy. Well, then, your only alternative is to have him enlisted. The army is the best school for discipline, especially for youngsters like him. Why, when I stop to think of his treatment of Miss Trehayne, it seems damnably shocking—let us retire or I shall loose my temper.   Exeunt EDDY *and* LUNDY, L. U. E.

Enter ROBERT *with* MRS. DE MORI *and* ROWENA, *laughing*,
R. U. E.

Mrs. De M. (L.) And you pretend you are a coward?

Rob. (C.) I confess it—I have not the courage to engage in this war against the South.

Mrs. De M. How strange, a Northerner like you should be in sympathy with your foe—for are we not foes, since we no longer recognise your authority?

Rob. I would much prefer, with your permission, to leave the right to discuss that point with the statesmen who urged on the war. (MRS. DE MORI *smiles and goes up stage*, C.)

Row. Do you know, Robert, you unjustly accuse yourself when you say you are a coward?

Rob. How do you know?

Row. Because no woman could love a coward.

Rob. Do *you* love *me?*

Row. No, no, but if you are a coward—why, yesterday when we were out boating, and the strong tide nearly capsized our boat, you acted with a coolness, courage, and presence of mind that saved our lives.

Rob. That wasn't courage—it was the fear of an accident. I am too fond of living to lose my life.

Row. Yes, but when my horse took fright, and was galloping at a wild speed, you, at the risk of being trampled to death, seized and stayed him; you did not seem to prize your life much then.

Rob. Because my life without yours would be valueless. I am fond of life, because I am young—have health and hope; I love the broad and open sea, the green fields, the waving trees, the broad expanse of sky and breezy air. The world with me is filled with life and beauty, but without you its light and sunshine would be gone.

Mrs. De M. (*Advancing down* C.) Ahem! where is your father, Mr. Eddy?

Rob. Do you wish to see him? (*To* ROWENA.) Will you give to me, the rosebud in your hair.

Row. It is yours. (*Gives it.*) You will not give it away?

Rob. No. (*To* MRS. DE MORI.) I will find my father on the instant. (*Starts to go, but is detained by* ROWENA.)

Row. Nor exchange it?

Rob. Only for one thing on earth more precious.

Row. And what is that?

Rob. Yourself.   *Bows and* **Exit L. U. E.**

Mrs. De M. (*Going to* ROWENA. Rowena! that young man loves you.

Row. (*Coquettishly.*) Does he?

Mrs. De M. You know he does.

Row. I know something more.

Mrs. De M. And what is that?

Row. I love him.

Mrs. De M. Rowena, be advised in time—such an attachment cannot but lead to disappointment and unhappiness.

Row. How so?

Mrs. De M. Mr. Eddy informs me that he is to marry a Miss Bertha Trehayne of New York. The lady, in her own right, is said to be worth a hundred thousand dollars.

Row. And Robert informs me he would not wed her if she had ten times a hundred thousand dollars.

Mrs. De M. Rowena! have you ever had to doubt my desire for your welfare—my love for you?

Row. Never! never!

Mrs. De M. Then, for reasons which you some day may learn, crush any growing attachment for Robert Eddy ere it be too late.

Row. I am afraid it is now too late.

Enter EDDY L. U. E., *accompanied by* ROBERT.

Eddy. (*Shaking hands.*) Delighted to see you—this is indeed a pleasure. Ah! by the bye, there was some talk at Mrs. Berry's the other evening, of your going away ; is it true?

Mrs. De M. Yes ; we leave for the South in a few days.

Eddy. I regret to hear you say so. But how are you going to cross the lines just now? Had you not better stay here awhile longer? A settlement of affairs between North and South may be consummated in a short time, and then travel will be more easy.

Mrs. De M. I fear there would be a greater danger were we to remain here (*Looking towards* ROWENA *and* ROB. *who are up stage* C., *in earnest conversation*); besides, I have received an order signed by the President, granting us the required permission.

Eddy. (*Aside, going* L.) I quite readily understand the motive of her sudden departure. No better favor could she afford me than this.

Rob. (*Aside to* ROWENA.) I must pack up my traps.

Row. You—for what?

Rob. To go South.

Row. (*Amazed.*) South! wherefore!

Rob. Because you are going.

Enter FRITZ, L. C., *at back.*

Fritz. (*Going to* MRS. DE MORI.) Dere vas two shentlemens dot vas vant to speak mit you, Mrs. De Mori. Von vas foreign, because he speak French, and der oder vas not, he speak Irish.

Mrs. De M. (*Surprised.*) Who can they be, I wonder?

Fritz. Dey vas very sorry dey sait, to follow you here, but dey vas particular to speak important business mit you.

Eddy. You will see them here, Mrs. De Mori. (*To* FRITZ.) Admit them.

Fritz. (*Going.*) Shust so, admit them.

Exit FRITZ, L. C. *at back.*

Eddy. (*To* ROBERT *and* ROWENA.) Will you come into the conservatory? (*Pointing* R. H. *of stage.*) I have received a fresh supply of plants this morning, and would like your opinion very much in relation to them. Shall we go?

Row. With pleasure.

Eddy. This way then—(*Going off*, R. U. E.)

Rob. (*Taking* ROWENA'S *arm.*) This way suits me best.

Exit, with ROWENA, L. U. E.

Mrs. De M. (*Going to ottoman* C., *in thought*) I wonder who these interviewers are (*Sitting*) that follow me here, and what their business is?

Enter GREENVILLE *and* BULLAY, L. C., *at back; they bow to* ROWENA *as she goes off.*

Bull. (L.) Greenville, vare fine girl.

Green. (C.) Hang the girl!

Bull. Hang ze girl—hang yourself.

Green. Devil a bit will I hang myself.

Bull. And I shall not hang ze girl.

Green. Very well then.

Bull. Vare well then—Greenville, are we not friends—vat you call——

Green. Partners. Yes. (*They shake hands and come down* C.)

Bull. (L. C.) Pardonnez moi [par-do-nay moo-ah] madame, for this—what is de word—this——

Green. (L.) Intrusion.

Bull. C'est bon [say bong]—intrusion.

Mrs. De M. Your business, sir?

Bull. My business—I may say, our business; for the firm of Greenville and Bullay——

Green. New York agents for the Mexican gold mine, known as La Creole—that is, we represent the parties who wish to purchase it.

Bull. Ze business with you, is to make—to make—inquiries—permit me—Charles De Mori wish to sell ze gold mine La Creole in San Alonzo, Mexico. Ze people ve represent vish to learn from you if his title and right is valid.

Mrs. De M. If I understand you rightly, my brother, Charles De Mori, has offered to dispose of the gold mine La Creole, and you are likely to become its purchasers.

Green. Yes ; in the interest of others, however.

Bull. Before buying it we, of course, vant to inquire into the title. (*Producing will from pocket.*) Now here is a copy of the vill of your uncle—a strange vill.

Green. A mighty strange will, to say the least.

Bull. He must have been—vat you call—out of his filbert.

Green. No, no,—off his nut. (*Tapping his head.*)

Bull. Ah, yes !—off ze nut.

Mrs. De M. (*Rising.*) My brother has no right to sell the La Creole gold mine, for it is the property of my child. (*Xing to* R.)

Green. (C.) But by this will, I see your uncle bequeaths the estate to your child, should it be a son ; but if a daughter, the property in full, goes to your brother. You have but one child.

Mrs. De M. You are right, sir.

Bull. Zat is ze daughter. Ah, ze property, you see, goes to ze brother, madame.

Mrs. De M. No, sir, but to my son.

Bull. A son ! You have but one child, and zat is ze daughter.

Green. True ! How can you then, madame, have a son?

Mrs. De M. (*Xing to* C.) Listen to me, sir. You would purchase this property ; and it is only an act of common justice to tell you why I dispute my brother's right to it.

Bull. (L.) C'est bon. Proceed ; we are all—all prevention.

Green. Attention.

Bull. Ah, yes,—attention.

Mrs. De M. (*Sits on ottoman.*) When but a mere girl, I was married to a young Northern gentleman, but without the consent or knowledge of my relatives. That marriage was discovered, and, through a diabolical intrigue consummated by my brother, my husband was sentenced by the Mexican Government to hard labor and solitary confinement for life. He did not long survive his sentence, for he became an easy victim to consumption. Shortly before the birth of my child, my uncle was seized with a mortal illness, and upon his death-bed sent for and forgave me. He died in my arms, leaving the will to which you allude, bequeathing the property owned by him in Mexico to my child, should it prove to be a male, and to my brother should it prove a female. A few weeks afterward the child was born.

Green. And it proved to be a girl.

Mrs. De M. On the contrary, it was a boy—the just and rightful heir to the La Creole gold mine.

Bull. Vonderful atmosphere is New York weather! How come de boy born in Nashville, to be changed in New York to a girl? Does dose things happen vare often in dis part of ze country ?¦

Mrs. De M. Simple enough when you understand it. The young lady, whom you no doubt have seen with me, is my adopted daughter. I am very reluctant to speak upon this subject, but my duty compels me. Now, sir, when my child was born, I knew that my brother intended to destroy its life if a boy; and when it proved a son, to save its life I caused it to be changed for that of a friend's who gave birth to a female child about the same time. (*Rises and goes up stage* C., *but returns down.*)

Green. (*Xing to* BULL., *aside to him.*) Just what we were told. We must be careful.

Bull. You right, Greenville. (*To* MRS. DE MORI.) Your son, madame, vare is he now? Is he living or dead? If living, ze estate is his ; if dead, your brother can sell ze property to us.

Mrs. De M. With the necessary proof of his identity, he was confided to an old pensioner of our family, named José Massini, a Mexican by birth, who, however, most shamefully betrayed his trust.

Bull. And killed ze child.

Mrs. De M. Such, I believe, was his intention ; but I have discovered that my boy was saved, and brought here to New York.

Bull. But, parbleu, [par-bluh] where is he?

Mrs. De M. That I have yet to discover. But I have told you sufficient; and I warn you that if you purchase this property, it will be at your own risk. Good morning.

Bows and **Exit** R. C., *at back.*

Bull. Greenville, mon cher, (mong share) what is it zat we shall do?

Green. Wait, and keep our eyes open. The property is very valuable, which Charles De Mori sells ; first, because his title to it isn't good, and secondly, because the specimens shown from it are virgin gold.

Bull. Oh! if we can only find out for sure if this child is dead or alive, then we would know what to do.

Green. Yes.   How can we find out?

Bull. I say, if——

Green. And I say, how? (*This is worked up, repeated to climax.   They appear about to strike each other and then shake hands.   Same business throughout play.*)

Bull. Oh! go to ze—ze—devil——

Green. Not much. (*Placing fingers to lips.*)   Hush! some one is coming.

Bull. Ah! (*To* GREEN.)   We are friends?

Green. Yes ; look (*Pointing* L. U. E.) there.

Bull. It's the young lady, and young Eddy, her sweetheart. Ah! she make my heart jump.   Oh, if she was mine! I—here into the——

Green. The conservatory——

Bull. And keep our eyes and ears open, like a couple of—of——

Green. Damned rascals.

Bull. C'est bon—dam rascasals ; for you dam rascasal— you, not me. (*Business above repeated.*)

Green. I said we——

Bull. Oui, (oo-ee) I know, and I said you.

Green. Don't insult me.

Bull. I—you insult me—but sacré! (sack-ray.)—I—but dere, let us be friends—have a cigarette.

Green. No!   You have a cigar.

Bull. You know I only smoke cirgarettes.

Green. And you know I only smoke cigars. (*They quarrel as before.*)   Very well, are we friends?

Bull. We are. (*As they are going* R. H.—*pointing off* L.) There is the girl zat I love.

Green. (*Looking off* L. C. *at back.*)   And there is the woman that I fear, my wife. (*Staggers.*)

Bull. Your wife!   Vere?

Green. (*Pointing off* L. C. *at back.*)   Coming here—the more I run away from her, the harder she runs after me.

Bull. (*Throwing kiss off* L. C.)   Ah! ze woman zat I love.

Green. Oh, you can have her ; I'll not get jealous.

Bull. Vere well ; I'll speak to her—by and bye.

Exeunt both into conservatory R.

Enter MRS. GREENVILLE L. C. *at back, accompanied by* FRITZ.

Mrs. Green. (*Coming down* C. *excitedly, with* FRITZ.) Do you mean to say, sir, my husband is not here? Why I saw him enter this house an hour ago. Here take this dollar (*Gives him a dollar.*) and answer my question.

Fritz. Vat question would you have mit me?

Mrs. Green. Well! Have you forgotten already what I asked you?—where's my husband?

Fritz. (*Confused.*) Your husband? Yaah,—vot you vant mit him?

Mrs. Green. For what does a woman usually want her husband?—he's run away and left me, and a beautiful cottage in Plainfield, New Jersey; with the rent unpaid, the baker, grocer, and butcher bills to pay, and the gas cut off.

Fritz. Your gas cut off? Nein, dey could never cut off your gas, it's natural. (FRITZ *looks up stage and sees* GREENVILLE *looking out from conservatory.*)

Mrs. Green. I could have forgiven him for these trifles; had he not tried to get a divorce from me.

Fritz. Dot vas bad.

Mrs. Green. Yes; and he came home intoxicated two days ago, and broke up the furniture, and then deliberately accused me of having—of having——

Fritz. Been drunk yourself?

Mrs. Green. No! of having imbibed in colors while he imbibed in spirits—in short, he says I am too extravagant in dress. Do you think so?

Fritz. Dere is a great deal of stuff in your skirt, but dot's the fashion, I suppose. (*Looks up stage towards conservatory.*)

Mrs. Green. (*Looking up stage*; GREENVILLE *disappears from view.*) Who's in that conservatory?

Fritz. No von, except der vorms und slugs.

Mrs. Green. Come, answer my question and I will make it another dollar.

Fritz. Vat question?

Mrs. Green. What question!—Are you crazy?—where's my husband?

Fritz. (*Looks up stage;* GREENVILLE *appears at conservatory, holds up five dollar bill, and motions* FRITZ *not to tell his where-*

2

abouts.) Vell, if you come mit me, I see vere your husband be. (*going up* C.) Follow me.

Mrs Green. That I mean to do. I intend to traverse the entire breadth of the land to find my other half, and when I do, I'll—I'll——

Fritz. Vat?

Mrs. Green. What? I'll—are you a married man?

Fritz. Nein!

Mrs. Green. Then I'd rather nor tell you.

Exeunt *both* L. C., *at back.*

Enter ROBERT *and* ROWENA, *arm in arm,* L. U. E.

Row. (*Sitting on ottoman,* C.) And you intend to follow me South?

Rob. (*Leans over her* R. *of ottoman.*) Aye! and to the end of the world.

Row. But how can *you* cross the lines?

Rob. After the manner intended by you. I'm sure my application for the required order will not be refused. However, should it be refused, I shall hold you as a hostage of war, and make you my wife.

Row. Your wife? (*Rising in a dreaming manner.*)

Rob. Yes, my wife, for I love you, love you more than it is in words to express. You have brought light and sunshine into my life, and the most waste and barren spot in all the world would be a paradise if shared with you.

Row. How—how shall I answer you?

Rob. By saying, yes.

Row. I dare not; my mother has warned me.

Rob. (*Amazed.*) Warned you of what?

Row. I scarcely know. There is some mystery, but I do know her never failing tenderness and love, and it is my duty to consult her before I answer you.

Rob. Be it so, but I could not bear to hear you answer no. See, here is the rose you gave me; if you will stay—if you will become my wife, tell me I may keep it; but if you are to crush the dearest and the highest hopes I have, ask me for the rose back again.

Row. I will, and within the hour.

Rob. But will you not tell me, if the answer rested alone with you, could you love me?

Row. Robert, I——

Enter EDDY, L. C., *at back.*

Eddy. Miss Rowena! (*Coming down* C.) Your mamma is ask-ing for you.

Row. Where is she, sir?

Eddy. In the Blue room.

Row. I will go to her. (*Starts to go, followed by* ROBERT.)

Eddy. (C.) A moment, young man. I wish to speak to you.

Rob. Yes, sir. (*Leads* ROWENA *to* L. U. E., *and returns down* L. C.) Remember the rose.

Eddy. Now, young man, you are falling in love with that young lady.

Rob. No, father, I am not. I have fallen, and so deep that I can never get out again.

Eddy. But you will have to.

Rob. Impossible!

Eddy. Not when I command you?

Rob. Pardon me, father, but in the choice of a wife every man has a right to judge for himself.

Eddy. Do you dare to dispute my right! When I asked why you did not enlist in the army, you said your sympathies were with the Southern side, and though your utterance gave me pain, I for-gave you. Now, in answer to my second demand, you again refuse to do my bidding.

Rob. Sir! I love Rowena.

Eddy. Confound it! You will at once give up all hopes of this lady, if you are an honest man.

Rob. If I am an honest man! I *am* an honest man.

Eddy. Do you think it honest to marry a woman under false pretences? to find out afterwards that you are not what you seem, but a penniless, nameless man.

Rob. Father!

Eddy. Do as I wish, and you remain a gentleman. Refuse, and you become a beggar. What's your answer; will you give her up?

Rob. I can not.

Eddy. Then my duty as a gentleman compels me to tell you—

to prevent you from deceiving this lady—that the name you bear, the position you hold, you have no right to. You are not my son——

Rob. Not your son!

Eddy. No sir; but the creature of a questionable alliance.

Rob. 'Tis false! This is but a foul and dastard insult, and one that shall not go unavenged. (*Seizes* EDDY, *and is about to strike him, when the latter throws him off.*)

Eddy. How dare you attempt to strike me! There, (*Points to chair,*. R.,) be seated, and listen before you pre-judge me. Remember, your own obstinacy forces me to tell you the whole—the bitter truth. (*Sits on ottoman,* C.) Twenty years ago, while travelling through Mexico, I passed a day at Puento Rio; as I left my hotel at night en route for home, I was accosted by a man I had met before—José Massini, a peon. He had a child in his arms, wrapped beneath his cloak, and he begged me, in the name of humanity, to take it and save it. I consented; I brought the child to New York, and having no wife, no children of my own, I adopted, educated, and made a gentleman of him. (*Rises.*) You, Robert, are that child.

Rob. A foundling! Oh, why was I not left to perish! Better have remained within the confines of my lowly birth than lived for such a bitter hour. Better have been the humblest wretch on earth than to be lifted up to fall again like this. Oh, Rowena! Rowena! you are lost to me, indeed　(*Crosses to chair* L.)

Eddy. You now understand why you must give the lady up; that if you, a child of circumstances, were to marry the daughter of an aristocratic family, you would, perhaps, bring shame and disgrace upon her. I should never have told you this but for your recklessness and obstinacy.

Rob. But have you no papers that would lead to the discovery of my birth, or any clue whereby something definite could be reached, so that I may know the proper station of my life.

Eddy. I have in my possession a certain packet, the contents unknown to me, which I have given my word shall not be placed in your hands till you are of age. On your twenty-first birthday— a few months hence—it shall be given you.

Rob. Mr. Eddy.

Eddy. Nay, Robert, call me "father" still.

Rob. No, sir. I will not bear a name to which I have no right; nor will I further accept the wealth and position I thought were mine. To-day my life begins—one favor alone I ask; go to Rowena—for I have not the courage nor the heart ;—Tell her—as you have have told me—all. Tell her also that if she can still love the nameless outcast—if she will wait for me in confidence and trust—I will win a name and position for myself.

Eddy. I will. Come with me.

Rob. No! my brain's bewildered, and I must think. (*Drum and fife band heard in the distance, playing " The Girl I left Behind Me," piano.*)

Eddy. (*Up stage.*) Poor boy! Well, it is better that he should know; he's a fine fellow, and I wish I were his father.

Exit, L. C., at back.

Rob. (*Looking off* R. C. *at back.*) What are those? Hum—recruits marching to the steamboat landing. (*After pause.*) I'll walk down and watch them. Rowena, give me but one smile, one word of encouragement and hope, and I'll win a name you shall not blush to bear. <div align="right">Exit, R. C. <i>at back.</i></div>

March ceases. **Re-enter** GREENVILLE *and* BULLAY *from conservatory* R. *They come down stage.*

Bull. (C.) Sacré bleu! [sack-ray bluh] what a discovery! Just think, the heir to von of the richest gold mines in Mexico, here and tinks he's penniless.

Green. (L. C.) And doesn't know it.

Bull. A millionaire in his own right!

Green. And doesn't know it.

Bull. His mother in the house!

Green. And doesn't know it.

Bull. And will not. Oh, what a chance! If we were to buy the property—it vas cheap—and this young man were to have some accidents and were to die, to—to what you call—knock over the pail vid his foot?

Green. Kick the bucket.

Bull. C'est bon—kick ze bucket.

Green. Where has he gone? (*Goes up stage* C., *looking off* R. C. *at back.*)

Bull. (*Following* GREENVILLE *up stage.*) Let us vatch and

see.   His life is vorth too much.   Poor fellow! the vorld is very
hard upon him, and ve vill——

Green. Send him to a better one.

Bull. You shall send him.

Green. No, you.

Bull. I say zat you! (*Quarrel as before.*) Do you not vant ze
property?

Green. And are you not in love with the girl, who doesn't want
you?

Bull. Sacré bleu! like your wife, who prefer running after ze
man of men——

Green. My wife loves me, you French frog!

Bull. Is zat so, you Irish hound? (*Quarrel as before.*) Ah!
we are friends again—some one is coming.

Exeunt into conservatory, R.

Enter MRS. DE MORI and ROWENA, L. H., at back.

Mrs. De M. (*Coming down* C.) And now, Rowena, you know
all.   Now, since you are a child of strange circumstances, in
justice, you must not marry this gentleman, to whose position your
own humble origin would be a constant reproach.

Row. (*Down* L. C.) But, why, oh, why was I not told before—
before it was too late to crush my love—before my heart was
broken! (*Sinks on ottoman and weeps.*)

Mrs. De M. Heaven knows child, I have acted for the best ; and
I should not have told you now but for the visit of these agents.

Enter EDDY, L. U. E., and crosses to MRS. DE MORI while speaking.

Eddy. Madam, at the request of Robert, whose attachment to
your daughter——

Mrs. De M. Stay, Mr. Eddy, in order to avoid any unnecessary
pain, or useless explanation, let me at once say that any engagement between your son and my daughter is out of the question.
(*Xing down to extreme* R.)

Enter ROBERT, R. C., at back.

Rob. (*Aside, up stage.*) Mr. Eddy here?—then he has told all.

GREENVILLE and BULLAY Enter and remain at back.

Eddy. (C, *to* MRS. DE MORI.) You will pardon me—but
Robert——

Rob. (*Coming down* L. C.) Will speak for himself—and to Rowena alone.

Mrs. De M. (R.) Be it so. (*Xing to* ROWENA.) Rowena, you know your duty. (*Goes up stage, but returns down* C.)

Eddy. (*Aside to* ROBERT.) Remember, Robert, this is my final decision; either you consent to marry Miss Trehayne, or you quit my house. **Exit, R. U. E.**

Rob. (*To* ROWENA.) You have heard all?

Row. (C.) All what?

Rob. (L. C.) This sudden change from a position of honor and affluence to that of a person without name or parentage.

Row. (*Aside.*) He knows all. (*Aloud.*) Yes; I have heard.

Rob. Ah! and your answer?

Row. Do you still require it?

Rob. Yes. When I spoke of love, I little dreamt it was the love of a person without name or parentage.

Row. (*Aside.*) Ah! then he knows all, and merely renews his offer from mistaken honor. I will not be a blot on his name.

Rob. Rowena, your answer.

Row. Give me back the rose.

Rob. Ah! (*Kissing it, and gives it to her.*) As with that flower, so may your memory of me fade and wither. Good-bye, and for ever. (*Turns slowly up stage.*)

Row. Good-bye. Oh, mother! mother! take me away. (MRS. DE MORI *catches* ROWENA *as she faints, and leads her off*, L. U. E. ROWENA *drops flower, which Robert picks up.*)

Rob. She has gone from out my life forever. Alas! in this great wide world I am friendless and alone. (*Military music heard, piano in the distance, playing "Rally 'round the Flag."* ROBERT *stands transfixed to the spot a moment. The music is worked up to forte at the close of the act.*)

Enter LUNDY, R. C., *at back, accompanied by* EDDY.

Rob. Colonel, the proposition you made me is accepted—I offer myself as a recruit.

Lundy. (R. C.) And you are accepted.

Eddy. (L. C.) Robert! go not thus from me—stay! I implore you——

Rob. (C.) 'Tis too late—besides, my country needs my services.

Enter ROWENA, L. U. E.

Row. (L.)   Robert—Robert—where are you going?

Rob. (C.)   To the war—I am beggared in pocket and bank-rupt in love, and what better fate than food for powder!

Row. Stay, Robert—I do love you! (*Falls into his arms.*)

Lundy. There is no time to be lost—our bráve fellows are on the move.   Follow me.   Exit, R. C., *at back.*

Rob. (*Disengaging himself from* ROWENA.) Rowena, farewell! With your name upon my lips, your image in my heart, I go forth to win a name which you will be proud to bear.   Farewell! (ROWENA *swoons into the arms of* EDDY.)

Tableau.

ROBERT.   EDDY.
R. C., *at back.*   ROWENA.   L. C.
                              C.

GREENVILLE *and* BULLAY.
       R. H.

Quick Curtain.

ACT II.

Scene.—*Dilapidated Warehouse near Fredericksburgh, Va. At rise of Curtain, Music.* FRITZ *and* O'ROURKE *discovered near fire,* R. H. FRITZ *is dancing;* O'ROURKE *on sentry duty.*

O'Rourke. (*Near fire.*) You seem to be mighty clever with your legs.   It's practising ye are?

Fritz. (R.)   Vat for?

O'Rourke. To run away whin the inemy comes.

Fritz. Run avay! never!   I vas come to fight, und not to run avay, mine friend. (*Dances.*)

O'Rourke. What the divil are you doing?

Fritz. Trying to keep mineself warm.   I vas as cold as it vas by the North pole und I don't vish to freeze shust yet.

O'Rourke. (*Producing flask from pocket.*) Arrah, man, take a nip of this. (*Gives flask to* FRITZ.) It will warm you as nothing else will.

ROBERT heard without, R.

Robert. Halt!

O'Rourke. (*Seizes flask from* FRITZ.) Here comes the Sergeant!'' (*Puts flask back in pocket, and paces to and fro.*) The finest lad in the regiment.

Fritz. Ugh! Dere vas a mistake ven dey promoted him; it should have been me, not him. Don't I vas deserving of dose stripes?

O'Rourke. The divil doubt it—only the sthripes would be on your back.

Enter ROBERT, C. from R.

Rob. (*On entering.*) Keep a sharp lookout, boys. You won't have a long rest. This flag of truce for the burial of the dead will last only two hours, and then the engagement will be renewed.

O'Rourke. That's what we want, Sergeant

Exit, FRITZ, C. and L.

Rob. You can retire from sentry duty awhile, O'Rourke, and rest yourself. The chilly atmosphere hereabout makes the fire a rare treat. I suppose there is a scarcity of tobacco among you so I will share mine. (*Produces tobacco.*) It isn't much, but you are welcome.

O'Rourke. (*Taking tobacco.*) Thank you, Sergeant. Always good to us men, eh?

Rob. (*Going to table,* L. *down stage.*) There's no merit. We share the dangers, why not our tobacco?

O'Rourke. Oh, Sergeant, you're as modest as a woman and as brave as a lion. Faix! I'm glad you're an Irishman.

Rob. An Irishman!

O'Rourke. Bedad, yes. You're a Northerner. A Northerner is an Irishman, and an Irishman is a Northerner so they are—they arrived here from the same port.

Rob. The Colonel would not agree with you, were he here. He insists upon calling me a Southerner.

O'Rourke. (*Smoking pipe near fire.*) Sure, Sergeant, the Colonel has a prejudice against you, the divil only knows why.

Rob. I can not help that. (*Lights his pipe and sits at table.*) My heart is in the Northern cause, though I am a Southerner by birth. Unfortunately I am educated, and he hates education in the ranks. He opposed my promotion. I did not merit promotion, perhaps; but I do not deserve his dislike.

O'Rourke. Not merit promotion? Bedad! when you walked into the shot and shell as though they were green peas and led our men into the thickest of the fight, and brought back the wounded officer who otherwise would have perished, the whole regiment were unanimous in their praise of your gallantry. Indeed the Colonel was obliged to promote you.

Rob. Had there been any danger, I should not have done it.

O'Rourke. That's the fun of the thing. You believe yourself a coward, and you're the bravest man in the regiment.

Rob. You mistake. I do no more than any of my comrades would do. I neither dodge a shot, nor dread a bayonet, because I do not see any danger; but if I did, I'd run away.

O'Rourke. Faix! you would? But it would be after the rebels. (O'ROURKE *resumes sentry duty.*)

Rob. I have comrades here who prize their lives because they've those at home to love and live for; and who, in the long and silent nights, can dream of home, of tender looks, of sweet voices whispering constant love and hope; but I am nameless, friendless, and what matters it if I should fall in the heat of battle, or a stray shot should cause my death, when there is no one to regret my loss— no one to visit in time to come my silent tomb—

(*Drum call heard,* R. U. E.)

Enter COLONEL LUNDY, C. *from* R. *All salute.*

Lundy. (*On entering.*) Let the picket be re-enforced, and a sharp lookout be kept. The enemy, though quiet, are dangerous. This truce now in force affords no good reason to believe that mischief is not afoot. Before many hours you may look for some desperate fighting, or I'm no prophet. Where's the Sergeant in command?

Rob. (L., *advancing to him.*) Here, sir.

Lundy. (*Aside.*) It's strange that I should have taken a dislike to this fellow. Sir, your friend, Mr. Jerome Eddy, is dead.

Rob. I regret to say the news has already reached me.

Lundy. (C.) You behaved ungratefully to him.

Rob. Pardon me, Colonel, I shall ever remember him with gratitude and love. If I preferred fighting my country's enemy to marrying a woman I did not like——

Lundy. To fall in love with a Southern creole woman!

Rob. (R. C.) That was my affair, not yours.

Lundy. Ahem! I hope you will prove worthy of your promotion, and serve your country faithfully.

Rob. I hope so too, sir.

Lundy. Rather too important a position this, for a Southerner to hold.

Rob. I beg pardon. I am a Northern man.

Lundy. Oh! I thought you were a Southerner—a creole by birth.

Rob. I was a Southerner once, but I am now a Northern gentleman in all save birthright.

Lundy. We don't expect non-commissioned officers to be gentlemen.

Rob. But we expect the commissioned officers to be.

Lundy. (*Aside.*) Confound the fellow! (*Direct.*) Humph! Information has been received at headquarters, that there are spies within our lines.

Rob. Spies, Colonel?

Lundy. And that information of our numbers at each post, with drawings and plans, are being furnished to the enemy, and by a person in this regiment (*Looks at* ROBERT *with suspicion*). But let the traitor beware, for if we catch him, we'll shoot him down like a dog!

Rob. (*Aside.*) Why am I silent under this injustice? Is it respect for a brave man, or because I am a coward?

Lundy. You are silent, Sergeant.

Rob. I was hoping, Colonel, that the spy might be caught.

Lundy. And that he won't be found in the Northern lines?

Rob. Patriotism is too dearly cherished to find spies or traitors among our comrades.

Enter OFFICER C. *from* L., *with two packets.*

Officer. (*To Lundy.*) From the Commander-in-Chief, Colonel Lundy.

Lundy. (*Opens packet, reads.*) Eh! what is this? A packet of letters for you, Sergeant.

Rob. Thank you, sir. (*Takes packet and goes to table* L.)

Lundy. (*Reading,* C.) "Permit two Southern ladies to pass through your lines." What the devil do women want crossing the lines at such a time?

Officer. (R. C.) The brother of one of the ladies, I believe, died some hours since, and through influence with the Commander-in-Chief, she has been granted permission to pass to him with the next flag of truce for the wounded.

Rob. (*Seated at table, reading letter.*) Mrs. De Mori and Rowena here!

Lundy. I'd rather see the devil in the camp than a woman; but the present truce will shortly expire; they must wait for the next before they can pass. Now to inspect the enemy's outposts. (*Takes field glasses from table* L., *and* Exits C. *and* L.)

Rob. (*Rising and stopping officer as he is about to go off* C.) Officer, where are the ladies quartered?

Officer. At headquarters.

Rob. Thank you. (Exit OFFICER, C. *then* R.) I wonder whether they know that I am here? If they do, will they endeavor to see me before they cross the lines? And Rowena, does she care, I wonder, to know my fate—if I am living, or if I am lying beneath the sod, like many a better man with a bullet in his heart? (*Comes down* C. *in a pensive mood.*)

O'Rourke. (R.) What's the matter wid ye, Sergeant, you've a face as long as a docthor's bill.

Rob. Nothing, O'Rourke. *Goes to table* L., *aside.*) Now for the other packet. (*Opens it.*) As I supposed, from poor Mr. Eddy. (*Reads.*) "Is to be opened when twenty-one years of age." I am past that now. What is this? A certificate of birth of Robert Lundy, son of Mrs. De Mori, on October 13th, 1843, and properly attested, endorsed by a statement that for family reasons a female child had been substituted. Great Heavens! then Mrs. De Mori is my mother! (*Opens second document excitedly.*) I wonder what this contains?

O'Rourke. (*Speaking off at* C. *to* LUNDY.) Bedad, Colonel, you'd be picked off by the inimy like a pigeon from a trap, at any other time than this.

Lundy. (*Without.*) Have no fear for me, O'Rourke.

O'Rourke. (*Aside.*) A severe officer is the Colonel, but for all that he's a brave man.

Rob. Good! the second document, signed by Mr. Eddy, proving that his supposed son is the same child he rescued on the night of the 13th of October, 1843, from José Massini. These two documents make the chain of evidence complete. In Mrs. De Mori, I have found a mother—she is in the camp—but I can not leave my post—I have it—I will write to her, and enclose these precious proofs. They will be safer in her custody than in mine just at present. Who knows but I may fall in the next encounter. (*Writes at table in a nervous manner.*)

Enter GREENVILLE *and* BULLAY. C. *from* R.

Bull. (C.) Dis is ze place vare our friend Robert is—is——

Green. (R.) Stationed.

Bull. Stationed. I vish he vas stationed in the next vorld—vat you call——

Green. Under the ground——

Bull. Non, non.

Green. Sent to the devil.

Bull. C'est bon—sent to ze devil.

Green. Mrs. De Mori's brother is dead, and we have bought the property—but we can't hold it while this fellow (*Pointing to* ROBERT) is living.

Bull. Ah! he must die like many a better man.

Green. But, how? he's in every battle and in every charge—fights like a hero.

Bull. Ah! if I were behind him, and could put a bullet in his back. But no, he always comes out unhurt. Sacré! I hate him.

Green. Hush! Now tell me, have you the drawings of the redoubts and intrenchments ; and the number of men at each?

Bull. C'est bon—in the lining of my coat

Green. To-night they must be in the hands of the Confederates.

Bull. You had better take care of them.

Green. No—you—to have them found on me would be instant death.

Bull. Ugh! ze Irish is half ze lion, half ze cur.

Green. Ugh! French—half cat and half monkey.

Bull. (*Sees* LUNDY *who appears at* C.) Hush ! the Colonel! We are friends——

Lundy. (*Coming down* C.) Hullo ! what the devil do you want here ?

Bull. I vas looking at ze brave fellows you have ze honour to command.

Lundy. (*Aside.*) French ! (*Direct.*) Who are you ?

Green. The firm of Greenville and Bullay, general sutlers to the Northern forces.

Lundy. You mean a **firm** of swindlers, for such you are, and all who strive to grow rich in the same way. You sutlers are a curse to the soldiers ; you sell them inferior goods for which you demand exorbitant prices. I should like to hang a few of you.

Bull. Mais, parole d' honneur, [may, par-ol do-nuhr] Colonel, you are vare unkind. You give us vat you call—you call ze crooked nob.

Green. The straight tip.

Lundy. Now look here. Though you possess properly endorsed documents attested at Washington, I won't have you or any other strangers prowling about here ; we know there are spies within our lines, especially in this camp.

Bull. }
Green. } Spies !

Lundy. Aye! Spies, who are making plans of our intrench-ments and lists of our men. It is death to the rascals, when caught.

Bull. Monsieur [mo-syuh] ! I am a Frenchman, and ze glory of France is my life, my soul; my heart is full of honor, and swells at ze roll of ze drum, at ze call of ze bugle ; and I vill fight, if necessary, wiz courage for ze flag of my adopted country ; my enemy I vill tread under my heel—I vill stamp upon him, and crush him. I vill shoot, I vill slay, I vill kill ze enemy of my adopted country. (*Crosses* L. H. ; *bugle call to arms ; drum calls till* LUNDY *goes off.*)

Lundy. Sergeant !

Rob. (*Still writing.*) Yes, Colonel.

Lundy. What are you doing?

Rob. Writing a letter, but I have finished now. (*Seals letter.*)

Lundy. Follow me.

Exit LUNDY, *followed by* ROBERT.
O'ROURKE *pacing from* R. *to* L., *without* C.

Bull. (*Xing to* GREEN.) 'Tis he! and there he goes—the man whose death will bring us fortune. Oh, I will give you von hundred times its weight in gold for ze bullet zat finds its vay to his heart!

Green. Then make the offer to some one who wants the job, as I don't care to undertake it.

Bull. Hush! we must get rid of these dam papers, and, seconde, ve must get rid of him.

Green. He was writing a letter at that table, to some one. To whom could it be, I wonder?

Bull. Ve vill know ; it's still on ze table.

Green. How can you get it! (*Points up to* O'ROURKE.) If you take it you will be seen.

Bull. Vare easy. You speak with ze sentry and I vill steal ze letter. (GREENVILLE *goes up stage* C., *and is about to speak to* O'ROURKE *when he paces off* R. GREENVILLE *returns down stage just as* BULLAY *takes letters from table.*) A packet of letters for Mrs. De Mori!

Green. What is to be done?

Bull. Ha! ze vay—while I vatch ze sentry, steal ze letters out, and put zese in de envelopes, (*Gives him papers out of inside coat pocket.*) Zat vill be vat you call fall over ze partridge?

Green. Tumble to the game. (BULLAY *goes up stage* C. O'ROURKE *appears.* BULLAY *stands in a position before* O'ROURKE *so as to screen* GREENVILLE, *who extracts letters from envelopes at table.*)

Bull. (*To* O'ROURKE.) Ah, mon ami [mong am-mee], ze veather is vare dam and chilly. Brandy is ze only remedy to prevent ze cold in ze body.

O'Rourke. That's a great spache for a Frinchman.

Bull. (*Producing flask.*) Some brandy. Vill you drink? (*During this time* GREENVILLE *is opening letters.*)

O'Rourke. Will I? (*Taking flask.*) Won't I! (*Drinks.*)

Bull. (*Sings.*) " For ve are," vat you call, "jolly good fellows, ve are jolly good fellows," etc.

O'Rourke. And so say all of us, hurrah! And so you are.

Bull. Here is good luck. (*Drinks.*) Encore, Monsieur soldat!
[ong-kor, mo-syuh sol-dah].

O'Rourke. Encore! Brandy is a song that deserves a double
encore. Here goes. (*Drinks;* GREENVILLE *by this time has
placed papers given him by* BULLAY *in envelopes, and re-seals
letter.*)

Bull. You seem to like it.

O'Rourke. Loike it! Ain't I traiting it loike a brother?

Bull. Ah, yes; brandy and vhiskey are second cousins of the
von family, and related vare closely to the Irish.

O'Rourke. Bedad, I won't have any more.

Bull. No, monsieur; you've emptied ze bottle. Ah, here comes
ze Sergeant! (O'ROURKE *resumes duty and* BULLAY *comes down
C., as* GREENVILLE *comes forward to meet him.*) Ze papers—ze
lettare.

Green. Are here! (*Gives papers and letter to* BULLAY.)

Bull. Good! Ah, mon cher Robert, your lettare is in my possession,—your life vill be also vare soon.

Enter ROBERT C., *quickly*.

Rob. (*Going to table,* L.) O'Rourke, run to headquarters, and
deliver this packet to the party addressed. (O'ROURKE *takes
packet, salutes and* Exits C., *and* R. *followed by* ROBERT.)

Bull. (R.) Now ve have spring ze mine. Ve must prepare for
von grand——

Green. Blow up.

Enter ROWENA C. *from* L.

Row. (*Entering.*) 'Tis here they said that I should find him.
Thanks to the flag of truce, else this pleasure would not be mine.
Dear Robert! (*Coming down* C, *pensively*,) how my heart leaps
at the thought of meeting him.

Bull. (*Seeing her.*) Ah! Zis is von grand plaisir [play-zeer].
My heart beat with joy to hear your voice once more.

Row. (*Retreating a step.*) Pardon me, sir, but——

Bull. (*Advancing to her.*) I will pardon you anything.

Row. You are the person, I believe, who purchased the La
Creole mine, and other property of the De Moris' in Mexico, well
knowing that he who sold them had no right to do so.

Bull. Oh, vy do you treat me so vare unkind? You are the lady of my heart, and yet ven I vould for von sweet smile "brave ze battle and ze breeze,"—I would go up in ze gold mine and down in ze balloon.

Row. Permit me to pass.

Bull. In my heart ze grand passion——

Row. (*Stamping foot.*) Permit me to pass, sir.

Bull. You will hear me?

Row. If you are a gentleman——

Bull. I am a Frenchman.

Enter ROBERT, C. from R.

Rob. (*Entering.*) Hullo! what's this?

Bull. Von lettle vord—(ROBERT *sees* ROWENA'S *face.*)

Rob. (C. *down stage.*) Rowena! Rowena! (*Rushes to her.*)

Row. Robert! (*They embrace and retire up* R.)

Bull. (*Going* L., *disgusted.*) Ugh! Sacré! I am vot you call——

Green. (*Who has followed him.*) Out of the hunt.

Bull. He cross my path. She gives—vot you call—ze frozen elbow.

Green. No, the cold shoulder.

Bull. I vill have my revenge. I vill soon—soon——

Green. Make it hot for him.

Bull. Make it hot for him, for I hate him.

Exeunt both C. and L.

Rob. (*Coming down* C. *with* ROWENA.) Dear Rowena, I have the pleasure of seeing you again, and the long and weary months of anguish and misery are forgotten.

Row. (R.) Oh, Robert! Why did you leave New York in anger, and the friends who loved you?

Rob. Did you not reject me—refuse my love, because of my altered position?

Row. No, Robert, no. It was because I myself had learnt I was not the daughter of Mrs. De Mori.

Rob. I have written to her; has she received my letter?

Row. No! but she will be here directly; she is most anxious to see you. How came you to be promoted? and what did you do to receive your Sergeantship?

3

Rob. I scarcely know. It was a cold gray morning in November, the ground heavy with frosty dew, and the air thick and misty with rain clouds ; the men were sleeping, everything about the camp was quiet and silent, when from the valley below a strange and muffled sound was heard, and then in the dawning light a thick grey mass of moving men was seen, and the enemy were upon us ; a shot was fired, the drums were beaten, the bugle called to arms, and in an instant the men sprang up to life and action. On came the enemy, and down went we to meet them, shoulder to shoulder, with a ringing Union cheer. Ah! how many a brave and noble fellow shed his blood that day upon bleak and barren fields, and left the hearts he loved to mourn him.

Row. But you, Robert, you——

Rob. I had no time to think, I had but to do, and with my comrades struggled to gain every available inch of ground, bayonet to bayonet, and foot to foot ; our officers were killed, the ground was covered with the dying and the dead ; and, overwhelmed by numbers, we were losing ground. My comrades showed signs of despair, when I rushed into their midst, and, with a desperate cheer of encouragement renewed their spirit, and led them on to victory.

Row. And did you think of me?

Rob. Your name was on my lips, and in my heart. I had a rebel down, a man who fought with desperate bravery throughout; there he lay helpless and fallen, my bayonet was at his heart—I looked into his defiant face, and there I saw——

Row. Mine?

Rob. Yes! yours—the same dark earnest eyes, the same expression.

Row. And you killed him?

Rob. No! spared him ; he was wounded and I brought him prisoner to the camp.

Row. Have you seen him since?

Rob. No. I was promoted on the field of battle, and have since been to busy to visit him. (*Drums, bugle, salute, heard off*, C.)

Enter LUNDY *and* O'ROURKE, C. *from* L. *accompanied by four soldiers ; they advance down stage*, L.

Lundy. (*Crossing to* ROBERT.) Sergeant, you are under arrest.

Rob. (C., *with soldiers* R. *and* L. *of him.*) I, Colonel! For what?

Lundy. Let your conscience tell you. (*To* ROWENA.) You must return to headquarters at once.

Row. But Robert! (*To* LUNDY.) Oh, sir, if he is in danger let me remain with him.

Lundy. Impossible! (*To* SOLDIERS.) Conduct the lady back.

, Row. But sir—(*Music, piano—continued.*)

Lundy. Silence! (*Aside.*) Hang it, my mother was a woman— (*Aloud.*) Well—well—say farewell and leave him.

Rob. Have no fear, Rowena, there is some mistake—good-bye.

Row. (*Going.*) Good-bye! (*Going up* C., *she looks back.* ROBERT *rushes to her, embraces her, and she* Exits *with* SOLDIERS C. *and* L.)

Lundy. (*To* SOLDIERS *who are escorting* ROWENA.) Bring back with you the prisoner, José Massini, taken by this man. (*Pointing to* ROBERT. *To* ROBERT.) Now to deal with you. I have received a communication to the effect that the papers we require are in a sealed packet, addressed to a Southern lady in the camp.

O'Rourke. (*Up* C. *to* ROBERT.) I hope there is no harm—there is the letter. (*Gives it to Lundy.*)

Rob. (L.) That is my property.

Lundy. (R.) Young man, a grave and terrible charge hangs over your head. Open that letter and clear yourself.

Rob. It is a private letter, and I deny your right to pry into its contents.

Lundy. Open that letter.

Rob. I decline.

Lundy. Beware, young man; you are suspected of an odious crime—of being a spy and a traitor to your country.

Rob. Colonel! such a charge is almost too absurd even for indignation—but I give you my word of honor, as a man, that the letter contains only information of a family nature.

Lundy. Once again, will you open it?

Rob. No!

Lundy. Then my duty compels me to do so. O'Rourke, open this letter and hand me the contents. (O'ROURKE *hesitates; he looks first at* ROBERT *then at* LUNDY.) Obey orders.

O'Rourke. (*Aside.*) Bedad, I must, though I'd rather not.

(*Music—opens letter, hands contents to* LUNDY, *retaining envelope.*)

Lundy. (*Reads.*) Ha! what are these? Go! (*To* O'ROURKE.) bring me the person to whom this letter was addressed. (Exit O'ROURKE, C. *and* L.) So, so, a plan of the intrenchments, and a list of the men.

Rob. I—I—did not place them there—there is some treachery.

Lundy. Treachery! aye! and you are the *traitor!*

Rob. 'Tis false! my honor is as stainless as your own.

Lundy. (*To* O'ROURKE, *who re-enters* C. *from* L.) Who gave this to you?

O'Rourke. (R.) The sergeant.

Lundy. Did it leave your hands before you opened it?

O'Rourke. Divil a moment, Colonel.

Lundy. (*To* ROBERT.) You hear! Oh, so young and yet so depraved! Were your crime less detestable, I could almost pity you.

Rob. I ask no pity—I demand justice.

Lundy. Then you ask for death—a death most disgraceful and revolting.

Enter MRS. DE MORI, C. *from* L.

Mrs. De M. (*Seeing* ROBERT, *goes to him and shakes hands.*) Robert!

Lundy. (R. MRS. DE MORI'S *back to* LUNDY.) Ah! you know the prisoner, madam?

Mrs. De M. (C.) The prisoner? (*Turns and sees* LUNDY.) What! my husband,—and alive!

Lundy. Louisa, my wife! (MRS. DE MORI *about advancing to him.*) Stand back! I have a stern and terrible duty to perform.

Enter SOLDIERS *with* JOSÉ MASSINI, C. *from* R.

José. (*Seeing* ROBERT *as he advances down* C.) The soldier who saved my life!

Lundy. Ha! you have more than a passing regard for this man. (*Pointing to* ROBERT.)

José. I have, for the consideration he extended to me.

Lundy. (C.) Your name?

José. (R.) José Massini. (ROBERT *and* MRS. DE MORI *start.*)

Mrs. De M. (L. C., *to* LUNDY.) One moment, as you value all you hold dear in life. José Massini do you know me?

José. (*After pause.*) Yes; Louisa De Mori, the daughter of the late Charles De Mori of Nashville, Tennessee.

Mrs. De M. 'Twas you who, twenty years ago, took away my son. Where is he?

José. I can tell you nothing. I have my duty to myself.

Lundy. How do you mean?

José. I am among enemies.

Lundy. You are among men, who will treat you with justice and humanity.

Rob. (*Advancing to* JOSÉ.) Speak the truth, sir, as much depends upon it.

Mrs. De M. Speak! There stands the husband who doubted my love.

José. He was misled by a forged letter.

Lundy. Ah!

Mrs. De M. And the child, our son. What has become of him.

José. He was adopted by a Northern gentleman.

Mrs. De M. His name?

José. Jerome Eddy ;—— lives at Fort Lee, New York.

Lundy. My son! my son! a traitor and a spy!

Mrs. De M. A spy and a traitor!

Lundy. Aye. (*Showing papers.*) Proved here beyond a doubt.

Mrs. De M. But you will save him?—your son?

Lundy. Were he twenty times my son, I have a duty to perform.

A bugle call, "the alarm," followed by roll of drums.

Enter ORDERLY, C., *gives despatch to* LUNDY, *and* Exits C.

Rob. Do not plead for me, mother; I am innocent. And whatever my fate may be, I can meet it like a man.

Lundy. (*To* SOLDIERS.) Take the prisoner back to his quarters.

Exeunt JOSÉ, O'ROURKE *and* SOLDIERS, C. *and* R.

Lundy. The attack has begun. (*To* ROBERT.) You are my son, and Heaven knows I would have taken you to my heart and loved you. But you stand dishonored in the eyes of man. The enemy have planted their flag on our outer battery—(*Bugle call; reports of cannon* L. H., *answered* R. H., *without* C.) A forlorn hope of volunteers are starting now to take it, and I would not see you die a traitor; the service is one of death. Go, then, and meet it like a soldier.

(Trumpet calls as before. Reports of cannon.)

Mrs. De M. No, no!

Rob. I will! (*Trumpets and reports.*) My honor is true and spotless as your own. But you, my father, doubt me. I'll seal its truth in death, or bring back a name you shall be proud to own. Farewell, mother! If I fall, tell Rowena how I died—wronged and misjudged! (*Embraces* MRS. DE MORI.) Farewell!

Exit ROBERT hurriedly, C. and R., (Bugle calls, roll of drums, and reports of cannon heard at intervals.)

Lundy. (*To* MRS. DE MORI.) I must to my post. After many years your truth and fidelity are proved. Let us not part in anger.

Mrs. De M. My son! You have killed him.

Lundy. He was dishonored.

Mrs. De M. 'Tis false!

Lundy. I am going into action, perhaps death. Say farewell.

Mrs. De M. Never! Bring back my son alive, or take a mother's curse.

Lundy. Be it so! The fate I sent him to, I myself will share. (*Rushes off* C., *and disappears* R. *Alarms as before, reports, etc.* MRS. DE MORI *swoons into chair* L., *near table.*)

Enter ROWENA C. *from* L. *followed by* BULLAY *and* GREENVILLE.

Row. (*On entering—much agitated.*) Robert! where is he?

Bull. (L. C. *up stage in front of her.*) Let me tell you. Your brave soldat is with ze forlorn hope.

Row. (C.) Ha!

Bull. (*Following her down stage.*) He vill die. He vill be shot.

Row. No! He will return.

(Trumpets again heard; reports as before.)

Bull. But not alive—you hear—he must have nine lives of ze cat. Ah! it varm my heart, to see him dead.

(Trumpets again heard; reports as before.)

Enter LUNDY C. *from* R. *agitated.*

Lundy. (*Down* C.) The battery is taken, and the flag down. (*A loud cheer heard without* C., *from* R. GREENVILLE *and* BULLAY *retire up at back*, L. H. MRS. DE MORI *revives, and* ROWENA *rushes to her.*)

Mrs. De M. (*Rising.*) My son!

Row. Robert, where is he?

Enter ROBERT, C. *from* R., *in an exhausted condition, followed by* FRITZ *and* SOLDIERS. *He staggers stupidly down* C.

Rob. Here! Mother—Rowena! (ROBERT *about to come down stage, when a flash of fire is seen at back, coming from without* C., *followed by reports of cannon; he staggers and falls lifeless on stage.*)

Mrs. De M. Heavens! he is dead! (*Swoons into the arms of* LUNDY.)

Tableau.

SOLDIERS.	SOLDIERS.		GREENVILLE *and* BULLAY.
up R. C.			L. C.
		FRITZ.	
		up C.	
		LUNDY *and* MRS. DE MORI.	
		L. C.	
SOLDIERS.	SOLDIERS.	ROBERT.	ROWENA.
R.		C.	L.

Quick Curtain.

ACT III.

Scene.—*Handsomely furnished drawing-room in* MRS. DE MORI'S *house, near Richmond, Va.*

At rise of curtain.—Enter FRITZ *and* MRS. GREENVILLE, C., *down steps.*

Fritz. (*Coming down* R. C.) You vill vate here, Mrs. Greenville; I vill tell your husband you vas come. (*Starts to go up* C.)

Mrs. Green. Just a moment, Fritz. (FRITZ *returns* R. C.) How came you to quit the army, and how is it I find you in the employ of a Southern lady?

Fritz. Dot vas strange mit you, eh? Vell I vill explain mineself. Ven I gots myself sick in the army I gots me a furlong, und stharted for mine home. The rebels surprised my side, und I thought it vas better to accept vork mit Mrs. De Mori, den risk my life by trying to get North.

Mrs. Green. (C.) A wise precaution, to say the least. (FRITZ *starts again up stage, but returns.*) Fritz! What is my husband and his partner, Mr. Bullay, doing here? (*Taking seat* L. *of table* R. C.)

Fritz. Shust as dey blease; dey vas bosses of der house, und especially dot vily Frenchman. Mrs. De Mori, vas no sooner found by her son, den he vas shot in the drenches—shot in der moment of his victory, und now dese lawyers, as dey say dey vas, claim dis place along mit der oder properties of der dead Charles De Mori. How in de vorld did you cross de lines, Mrs. Greenville?

Mrs. Green. By the same means as your mistress. Ah! a woman will make her way anywhere when she's in search of a husband.

Fritz. Dot is so—(*Looking off* L. 3 E.) Ah! here comes Messrs. Greenville and Bullay.

Mrs. Green. (*Rising.*) You need not announce me—that is not just yet. So sudden an announcement, I fear, would upset my husband's nerves; he is so delicate, you know—Come, Fritz, usher me into some place where I can observe his actions. I so like to pounce upon him suddenly—husbands, you know, admire that sort of thing.

Fritz. (*Xing to door*, R. 3 E.) Quick! in here; dey vas coming.

Mrs. Green. (*Xing to* R. 3 E.) Oh! when the war is over, won't I fix that husband of mine! Exit, R. 3 E.

Enter GREENVILLE *and* BULLAY, L. 3 E., *quarrelling*.

Fritz. (*Retiring up stage, unseen by them.*) Ah! shust in time.

Green. (*Coming down* C.) I tell you that you are a humbug.

Bull. (*Down* R. C., *excited.*) Is zat me you vill call von humbug? Ugh! Sacré bleu, I vill—I vill—blow your nose. (*Attempts to pull* GREENVILLE'S *nose.*)

Green. (*Stops him.*) No, you won't!

Bull. Oui! but I vill. (*They quarrel; seeing* FRITZ *up* C., *who is looking off* R.) Ah! we are friends. (*They shake hands. To* FRITZ.) Ah! Fritz, you no pass across ze lines to ze North? Ah! yes, you like ze South after all, especially Mrs. De Mori. Tell ze Madame, zat we vould feel a plaiser—zat is Messrs. Greenville et [ay] Bullay vould have ze honneur of an——

Green. Interview.

Fritz. Mrs. De Mori vas indispossible, but I vill tell her you would speak mit her.

Enter MASSINI C., *from* R., *down steps.*

Green. (*Advancing towards* MASSINI.) Ah! what news?

Massini. (*Down* C.) It was impossible to deliver your letter to General Lee. (*Returns letter to* GREENVILLE.) There is every indication of a surrender of the South. It is rumored, and the rumor comes from a reliable source, that Lee is about to offer his sword to Grant.

Bull. Mon Dieu! [mong dyuh] zat vill spoil all our little plans, eh, Greenville.

Green. Not my plans. (*To* MASSINI.) You are willing to serve us?

Massini. Why not? you offer to pay me well, and I am at your command.

Bull. Zat is vell. (*To* GREENVILLE.) Zis bizness must be quick if the report of the surrender be true. (*To* MASSINI, L. C.) And zis girl Rowena, she is your daughter?

Massini. No, the child of my brother, whose wife was an octoroon.

Bull. And no von knows zis?

Massini. No; the father and the mother both are dead.

Green. You do not intend to claim relationship with this young girl?

Massini. Not much. Her father, my brother bought her mother from me,—using trickery and subterfuge to accomplish his purpose, and I never forgave him. For twenty years I have felt the rankling thirst for vengeance.

Green. You serve our interest, and you shall have it.

Massini. Be it so. I have those about me who will aid in carrying out your plot, if their services be needed. (*Going.*) We shall be within call when you are ready. Addios!

Exit MASSINI, C. *then* R.

Bull. Ha! ha! Greenville, mon cher, we vin ze leetle game. We are safe within the Confederate lines. We have been well paid. Ve have claimed ze estate, and Robert—our bête noir [bayt noo-ar]—vas killed—vas dead. Just ven he vas found he vas lost. Ah, ve had vat you call ze thin squeal.

Green. A narrow squeeze of it.

Bull. Ze estate is ours. Vare are ze two papers zat prove ze change of children—ze identity of Robert?

Green. Here in my pocket.

Bull. Suppose zat I put zem in mine.

Green. Suppose that you don't.

Bull. Suppose zat I do.

Green. I'll see you hanged first.

Bull. Do you doubt my honneur?

Green. Do you doubt mine? (*They quarrel as before.*)

Bull. No, no, you von gentilhomme [zhong-te-yom].

Green. And you're another.

Bull. Ve vill keep up our rule to square up as we go. You shall keep ze von and I shall keep ze ozere.

Green. Very well. Here they are (*Produces papers and gives* BULLAY *choice.* BULLAY *takes one.*)

Bull. (*Examines paper.*) I have ze von zat certify to ze change of children.

Green. And I have number two, that certifies that Robert was that same child.

Bull. Ha! ha! Now Rowena, she will soon be mine. Oh, ze charmante girl!

Green. Bah! she doesn't care a straw for you.

Bull. Care a straw! she shall care ze whole hay-stack. Ugh! I vill pull your eye, I vill black your nose for you. You tink she not love me, because your vife make a fool of you vith running avay from you.

Green. You say that again!

Bull. Ha! ha! Your vife make a fool of you——

Green. Ah! (*As he turns on* BULLAY, MRS. GREENVILLE Enters, R. 3 E., *and comes between them.*)

Mrs. Green. (C.) You know better.

Green. The devil—my wife!

Bull. (*Retreating up stage.*) Sacré bleu! Ze leetle fat, fair and forty, I'm off. Exit C. *then* R.

Mrs. Green. And so, Mr. Greenville, I have found you!

Green. Yes, Mrs. Greenville.

Mrs. Green. Oh! if I could harrow up your feelings! but you haven't any. If I could touch your heart! but it is only a pumping machine. Oh! why did you leave the beautiful villa at Plainfield?

Green. (R.) Because the atmosphere was uncongenial.

Mrs. Green. (C.) Didn't I look after your comforts?

Green. Yes, you gave me bacon and cabbage, morning, noon and night.

Mrs. Green. Because I wished to make you a solid man. I suppose your coming home at three o'clock in the morning, drunk, was no annoyance to me. What did I do to comfort you, when you wanted to go to bed in this condition, with your boots on?

Green. Emptied the water jug over me.

Mrs. Green. Wasn't I kind to your friends?

Green. Yes, too kind when they were good looking young men.

Mrs. Green. Mr. Greenville!

Green. How about the distinguished looking individual, who always came when I was out? The fellow, who put on my dressing-gown, wore my slippers, drank my whiskey, and smoked my cigars?

Mrs. Green. Who told you so?

Green. Somebody who saw him.

Mrs. Green. Who?

Green. My friend and partner, M. Bullay.

Mrs. Green. Oh! oh! Of course he saw him?

Green. Ah!

Mrs. Green. And in the dressing-gown and slippers

Green. (*Xing stage, pulling his hair.*) Oh!

Mrs. Green. And smoking your cigars.

Green. Ah! and told me like a friend—good Bullay!

Mrs. Green. Of course, good Bullay saw all this! because he himself was the distinguished individual.

Green. What?

Mrs. Green. The villain tried to deceive me, and make a fool of you, and, fearing I should tell you, has made all the mischief. Greenville, I have been a true and good wife to you.

Green. Are you sure of it?

Mrs. Green. Quite sure.

Green. Then come to my arms. (*They embrace.*)

Mrs. Green. Patrick!

Green. Juliet!

Mrs. Green. François Bullay, is a scamp.

Green. He is.

Mrs. Green. And you're another. You come with me and I'll show you a letter in his own handwriting, proving his treachery to you—come—come—(*Pulling* GREENVILLE *along with her*, R. H.)

Green. Oh! oh! François Bullay—you then were the distinguished individual; but beware of the uprising of Ireland!

Mrs. Green. Patrick!

Green. Juliet! *Exeunt both*, R. 3 E.

Enter MRS. DE MORI *in mourning, with* FRITZ, L. 3 E.

Mrs. De M. (*Coming down*, C.) I will at all hazards leave this place; the presence of these two men, I can no longer endure.

Fritz. Vere vill you go?

Mrs. De M. Ah—where, indeed? I am utterly ruined by this war—my estate devastated—the crops destroyed—my houses burnt to the ground. Oh, where—where shall I find friends?

Fritz. Shust count on me, Mrs. De Mori, I vos one friend. I vould travel anywhere mit you.

Enter BULLAY, C. *from* R.

Bull. (*Down* L.) And anozzer in me. I vill serve you wiz mine heart—I vill help you wiz mine hand.

Mrs. De M. You have already proved your friendship, Mr. Bullay; it is the friendship of the serpent when he winds his coils round his victim. Friendship! the friendship of the adder.

Bull. If I am ze adder, mind I do not sting.

Mrs. De M. Go, Fritz. *Exit* FRITZ, R. 3 E.

Bull. You know, madame, zat I am ze owner of what was your propeity?—zat your son was shot—he vas killed?

Mrs. De M. (*Weeps.*) My boy—my brave boy!

Bull. Ah! ze tear is in your eye. I love Rowena; let her become my wife, zen ze property shall still be yours.

Mrs. De M. Never! Rowena your wife! I would rather see her in her grave. (*Xes to* L.)

Enter ROWENA, C. *from* R.

Row. (C.) Mother! what is this?

Mrs. De M. (L.) Nothing, my child.

Bull. (R. H.) I vait my answer from ze lady herself.

Mrs. De M. Rowena, my darling, this man dares to propose for your hand in marriage.

Row. Ah, does he not know?

Bull. I know zat ze young man you love is dead—is gone vare he nevare return, and ze love you gave to him I vould for myself.

Row. Robert! my brave, my noble-hearted Robert, how handsome, how bright and glorious he looked, how proud and happy as he bore the Union colors in his hand—oh, mother, mother, would that I could die! (*Sinks in chair* L.)

Mrs. De M. Hush, Rowena, hush, I too have my sorrow to bear.

Row. Mother!

Mrs. De M. He was a brave boy, he would have been your husband. And in your young lives, in your happiness, I should have found my own. No; you shall never be his. (*Pointing with disdain towards* BULLAY.) You have your answer. No!—

Bull. But I insist.

Row. Nay, mother, let me hear him. (*Rising.*)

Mrs. De M. Then, sir, be brief. (*Retires up stage* C., *and off* L. U. E.)

Bull. Ah! ze Mrs. De Mori, you love her, why not me?

Row. Love, Mr. Bullay, is created by love, and fostered by kindness, devotion, and self-sacrifice, not by threats and persecution.

Bull. My heart is kind, and I would not threaten you, nor persecute. But, oh! my love for you have changed my life. For you,

I can be as good as ze angels ; for you, I can be as bad as ze devils; for good or bad you can make me what you will.

Row. I have told you, sir, I have no love to give.

Bull. You gave it to a boy—a boy who know not how to prize ze jewel he had von and vas ze spy and ze traitor.

Row. 'Tis false ! how dare you malign the dead, and to me, who knew him the soul of honor?   He lived a blameless life, and died a soldier's death.

Bull. He was a spy.

Row. He was a man, and worthy to command a woman's love —I have no love for you. (*Xing to* R.)

Bull. (*Xing to* L.)   If you have no love for me, you will have no home for yourself, for Mrs. De Mori—she vill starve ; be my wife and save your mother—or she starve.

Row. (*To* C.)   Starve !

Bull. Oui, for ze property is now mine, not von ting does Mrs. De Mori own.   Ah, mon amie, von leetle vord of yours can save her.

Row. (*Aside.*)   She has been more than a mother to me, gave me years of tender watchfulness and love.   I owe my life and more to her ; and is she not the mother of Robert ?

Bull. I vate your answer.

Row. If what you say is true—if—if there be no other means to save her——

Bull. You vill be my wife?

Row. For her sake I—I——

Bull. Ah ! (*As he is about to take her hand,* MRS. DE MORI Re-Enters C. *from* L. *and comes down between them.*)

Mrs. De M. Never ! rather than accept the sacrifice, I would go and labor in the cotton-fields beside the negroes ; rather than see her your wife I would lay her dead at my feet !

Row. Mother !

Mrs. De M. Hush, child !   Come what may, with one sacred memory, one chain of love between us, we will starve together.

Bull. You vill not let her be my wife ?   Then she be my slave !

Mrs. De M. ⎫
Row.   ⎬ Your slave !

Bull. Oui ; ven zat your son Robert you change, you took ze

daughter of a slave—an octoroon, and I have bought all ze slaves on zat estate and Rowena vas von of them.

Row. (*Screams and falls on her knees*). No! no! you will have pity—mercy——

Mrs. De M. You will not enforce this claim?

Bull. I will—I do. (*Calls.*) José Massini!

Enter MASSINI, C. from L.

Mrs. De M. José, what means this?

Massini. (R.) Pardon me, Señora, M. Bullay bought all my slaves some time since, and the mother of Rowena was among the number.

Bull. And in ze bill of sale it gives me ze right to all ze unsold offsprings of ze vomen. Ah, madame, you can now understand my position.

Row. Oh, sir, have you no human feeling in your heart? (*Music—bugle, fife and drum distantly heard off* L. U. E.)

Bull. Ze von human feeling in my heart vas my love for you. I am your master now! Monsieur, isn't zis girl von of my slaves? Vasn't her mother your vife?

Massini. Yes; and the girl is yours.

Row. Ah!

Bull. Monsieur, take avay ze girl—my slave. You vill I hold responsible for her safety.

Massini. (*To* MRS. DE MORI.) Pardon me, Señora, I'm in this man's service. (*To* ROWENA.) Come.

Row. (*Kneeling.*) Oh, mercy! Look at my mother. She has lost a son, and in this great unpitying world has no one but me. We are two weak defenceless women. Ah! are you human? Are you a man?

Bull. Vat! a man? I wouldn't vant to marry you if I vas not. You may as vell go peacefully. You have no hope, no chance. You vould have been ze slave of Robert, but he is dead! (*Drum roll heard without,* C.)

Enter ROBERT, C. from L., in officer's uniform.

Rob. (*At* C.) No, alive, and if Rowena's a slave at all, she's mine! (MRS. DE MORI *and* ROWENA *rush to his arms.*)

Exit MASSINI, C. and L.

Mrs. De M. (R.) Tell me, my boy, how you were saved?

Rob. (C.) After the taking of Fredericksburg by the Confederates, I was removed to their hospital, where I remained under medical care, till the retaking of the town by our side. Ah, mother, I owe much to the Colonel for the restoration of my life. When he discovered I was not killed, as reported, he had me removed to his quarters, and in the crisis of my danger, nursed me back to life with a woman's gentleness.

Enter LUNDY, C. from L.

Rob. My father! (*Advancing to* LUNDY.)

Mrs. De M. My husband! (*They embrace.*)

Lundy. (C.) Louisa, you told me to bring you back your son and he is there. We are not youthful lovers now, and in the vale of life the two best words the human heart can repeat are "Forget"

Mrs. De M. And "Forgive." (*She gives her hand.*) You give me back my son, take back my love.

Lundy. I now see the injustice I have done the lad. He's a fine fellow. I have but one regret—one cloud, the spy's papers found in his possession, and I have promised the day he proves his innocence I will acknowledge him as my son.

Mrs. De M. And why not now?

Lundy. Because there is a cloud upon his honor, and until it is cleared I can not hold out my hand to him and say, Robert, my son.

Enter O'ROURKE, C. from L., down steps.

Lundy. (*Advancing to him.*) What news?

O'Rourke. (*Giving him sealed packet, which Lundy opens.*) This packet will, I am sure, answer that question.

Lundy. (*Reads document.*) Eh! The South has succumbed—Lee has surrendered to Grant—

Rob. Thank Heaven!—Ah, the cruel war will soon be at an end! (*Comes down* R., *leaving* ROWENA *up stage. To* BULLAY.) I've an account with you, sir, and I want a settlement now——

Bull. (R. H.) Avec moi [av-ek moo-ah]—and who ze devil are you?

Rob. (R. C.) Robert De Mori Lundy, the heir to the estates of Charles De Mori.

Bull. Ha! ha! You have no proof at all.

Mrs. De M. But I have! (*Producing paper.*) This very deed by which you would make Rowena your slave, proves Robert to be my son.

Enter MR. *and* MRS. GREENVILLE *and* FRITZ, L. U. E.

Rob. You cannot deny the authority of this document, which proves Mrs. De Mori's story.

Bull. No! no! But you cannot prove you are zat son. Zat paper proves nothing.

Lundy. (*Having read the paper.*) True! for this paper only proves that your child was a boy, and at its birth was exchanged for a female child, the daughter of a planter—Carlos Massini. This is no proof that you, Robert, are that boy.

Bull. Ha! ha! (*Xing to* L.) but you have not ze ozare proof.

Green. (*Coming down* C.) No, they haven't, but I have.

All. You!

Green. And here it is. (*Gives paper to* ROBERT.) Signed by Mr. Jerome Eddy, properly attested, and proving you, with the other documents, to be beyond a doubt, Robert De Mori Lundy. And more—José Massini confessed to me that this girl, Rowena, was not his daughter, but the daughter of honest, though humble white people, now deceased; therefore, the girl is a free woman.

Bull. Ah traitor!

Green. Square as we go. This is the distinguished individual's debt.

Bull. Oh! if I had your head in my hand, your heart under my heel——

Rob. Now, Mr. Bullay, we will settle up. These two documents were stolen from me in the camp at Fredericksburgh, and the hand that stole them was the spy's—yours was the hand, and you the traitor.

O'Rourke. (*Coming forward.*) Here's the envelope, Colonel, the papers were in. Arrah, sure the seal on it, looks as though it had been tampered with.

Rob. (*Seizing envelope from* O'ROURKE.) You're right, O'Rourke; the seal has been broken, and resealed with another.

Bull. (*Feigns surprise.*) Vith anozzer! Who's?

Rob. Who's? (*Comes down to* BULLAY, *suddenly breaks off seal from his watch chain and compares it with packet.*) Why, yours, (*Chord.*) M. Bullay. See the traitor!

Lundy. (*After examining it.*) It is so beyond a doubt. Robert, my son, your hand.

Rob. Father!

Bull. I've got into ze hot vater, and, sacré, it begins to boil.

Lundy. (R. C.) So you were the traitor, eh?

Bull. I and my partner—let him share ze honor, for we share as we go.

Lundy. No. For in consideration of the service he has just rendered, his life along with yours, is unforfeited. Now, go; quit this house instantly or I'll put you under arrest. Go!

Bull. Oui, monsieur; adieu, M. Greenville, ve have rowed in ze same boat, but ve von't be hanged by ze same rope.

Exit L. 3 E.

Martial music distinctly heard, piano, and worked to forte.

Mrs. De M. What's that?

Fritz. (*Coming down* R. C. *from* C. *where he has been looking off* R. U. E.) It vas der troops leaving the city.

Lundy. Ah, Louisa! this re-union of the North and South will be the means of re-uniting many like ourselves, who have been so long parted.

Rob. Yes, and redeem the honor of those, who stood "Between Two Fires."

Tableau.

MR. *and* MRS. GREENVILLE.

up R. H.

ROBERT *and* ROWENA.

C.

LUNDY *and* MRS. DE MORI.

L. C.

FRITZ.   O'ROURKE.

R.   L.

Curtain,

HELMER'S
ACTOR'S MAKE-UP BOOK.

A Practical and Systematic Guide to the Art of Making up for the Stage.

PRICE, 25 CENTS.

WITH EXHAUSTIVE TREATMENT ON THE USE OF THEATRICAL WIGS AND BEARDS, THE MAKE-UP AND ITS REQUISITE MATERIALS, THE DIFFERENT FEATURES AND THEIR MANAGEMENT, TYPICAL CHARACTER MASKS, ETC. WITH SPECIAL HINTS TO LADIES. DESIGNED FOR THE USE OF ACTORS AND AMATEURS, AND FOR BOTH LADIES AND GENTLEMEN. COPIOUSLY ILLUSTRATED.

CONTENTS.

☞ In ordering, please specify **Helmer's** Make-up Book. ☜

SAVED FROM THE WRECK.

A DRAMA IN THREE ACTS, BY THOMAS K. SERRANO.

PRICE, 15 CENTS.

Eight male, three female characters: Leading Comedy, Juvenile Man, Genteel Villain, Rough Villain, Light Comedian, Escaped Convict, Detective, Utility, Juvenile Lady, Leading Comedy Lady and Old Woman. Two Interior and one Landscape scene. Modern Costumes. Time of playing, two hours and a half. The scene of the action is laid on the New Jersey coast. The plot is of absorbing interest, the "business" effective, and the ingenious contrasts of comic and serious situations present a continuous series of surprises for the spectators whose interest is increasingly maintained up to the final tableau.

SYNOPSIS OF INCIDENTS.

ACT I. THE HOME OF THE LIGHT-HOUSE KEEPER.—An autumn afternoon.— The insult.—True to herself.—A fearless heart.—The unwelcome guest.—Only a foundling.—An abuse of confidence.—The new partner.—The compact.—The dead brought to life.—Saved from the wreck.—Legal advice.—Married for money.—A golden chance.—The intercepted letter.—A vision of wealth.—The forgery.—Within an inch of his life.—The rescue.—TABLEAU.

ACT II. SCENE AS BEFORE; time, night.—Dark clouds gathering.—Changing the jackets.—Father and son.—On duty.—A struggle for fortune.—Loved for himself.— The divided greenbacks.—The agreement.—An unhappy life.—The detective's mistake.—Arrested.—Mistaken identity.—The likeness again.—On the right track.—The accident.—"Will she be saved?"—Latour's bravery.—A noble sacrifice.—The secret meeting.—Another case of mistaken identity.—The murder.—"Who did it?"—The torn cuff.—"There stands the murderer!"—"'Tis false!"—The wrong man murdered. —Who was the victim!—TABLEAU.

ACT III. TWO DAYS LATER.—Plot and counterplot.—Gentleman and convict.— The price of her life.—Some new documents.—The divided banknotes.—Sunshine through the clouds.—Prepared for a watery grave.—Deadly peril.—Father and daughter.—The rising tide.—A life for a signature.—True unto death.—Saved.—The mystery solved.—Dénouement.—TABLEAU.

THE GYPSIES' FESTIVAL.

PRICE, 25 CENTS.

A MUSICAL ENTERTAINMENT FOR YOUNG PEOPLE. Introduces the Gypsy Queen, Fortune Teller, Yankee Peddler and a Chorus of Gypsies, of any desired number. The scene is supposed to be a Gypsy Camp. The costumes are very pretty, but simple; the dialogue bright; the music easy and tuneful; and the drill movements and calisthenics are graceful. Few properties and no set scenery required, so that the entertainment can be represented on any platform.

BETWEEN TWO FIRES.

A Comedy-Drama in Three Acts, by Thomas K. Serrano.

PRICE, 15 CENTS.

Eight male, three female, and utility characters: Leading juvenile man, first and second walking gentlemen, two light comedians (lawyer and foreign adventurer), Dutch and Irish character comedians, villain, soldiers; leading juvenile lady, walking lady and comedienne. Three interior scenes; modern and military costumes. Time of playing, two hours and a half. Apart from unusual interest of plot and skill of construction, the play affords an opportunity of representing the progress of a real battle in the distance (though this is not necessary to the action). The comedy business is delicious, if well worked up, and a startling phase of the slavery question is sprung upon the audience in the last act.

SYNOPSIS OF INCIDENTS.

ACT I. AT FORT LEE, ON THE HUDSON.—News from the war.—The meeting.—The colonel's strange romance.—Departing for the war.—The intrusted packet.—An honest man.—A last request.—Bitter hatred—The dawn of love.—A northerner's sympathy for the South.—Is he a traitor?—Held in trust.—La Creole mine for sale.—Financial agents.—A brother's wrong.—An order to cross the enemy's lines.—Fortune's Fool.—Love's penalty.—Man's independence.—Strange disclosures.—A shadowed life.—Beggared in pocket, and bankrupt in love.—His last chance.—The refusal.—Turned from home.—Alone, without a name.—Off to the war.—TABLEAU.

ACT II. ON THE BATTLEFIELD.—An Irishman's philosophy.—Unconscious of danger.—Spies in the camp.—The insult.—Risen from the ranks.—The colonel's prejudice.—Letters from home.—The plot to ruin.—A token of love.—True to him.—The plotters at work.—Breaking the seals.—The meeting of husband and wife.—A forlorn hope.—Doomed as a spy.—A struggle for lost honor.—A soldier's death.—TABLEAU.

ACT III. BEFORE RICHMOND.—The home of Mrs De Mori.—The two documents.—A little misunderstanding.—A deserted wife.—The truth revealed.—Brought to light.—Mother and child.—Rowena's sacrifice.—The American Eagle spreads his wings.—The spider's web.—True to himself.—The reconciliation.—A long divided home reunited.—The close of the war.—TABLEAU.

READY NOV. 15, 1888.

THE COURT OF KING CHRISTMAS.

PRICE, 25 CENTS.

A Christmas entertainment. The action takes place in Santa Claus land on Christmas eve, and represents the bustling preparations of St. Nick and his attendant worthies for the gratification of all children the next day. The cast may include as many as 36 characters, though fewer will answer, and the entertainment represented on a platform, without troublesome properties. The costumes are simple, the incidental music and drill movements graceful and easily managed, the dialogue uncommonly good, and the whole thing quite above the average. A representation of this entertainment will cause the young folks fairly to turn themselves inside out with delight, and, at the same time, enforce the important moral of Peace and Good Will.

ENTERTAINMENTS IN PREPARATION.

AN EVENING WITH DAVID COPPERFIELD.

THE JAPANESE WEDDING.

AN EVENING WITH THE PICKWICK CLUB.

SAVED FROM THE WRECK.

A DRAMA IN THREE ACTS, BY THOMAS K. SERRANO.

PRICE, 15 CENTS.

Eight male, three female characters: Leading Comedy, Juvenile Man, Genteel Villain, Rough Villain, Light Comedian, Escaped Convict, Detective, Utility, Juvenile Lady, Leading Comedy Lady and Old Woman. Two Interior and one Landscape scene. Modern Costumes. Time of playing, two hours and a half. The scene of the action is laid on the New Jersey coast. The plot is of absorbing interest, the "business" effective, and the ingenious contrasts of comic and serious situations present a continuous series of surprises for the spectators whose interest is increasingly maintained up to the final tableau.

SYNOPSIS OF INCIDENTS.

Act I. The Home of the Light-house Keeper.—An autumn afternoon.—The insult.—True to herself.—A fearless heart.—The unwelcome guest.—Only a foundling.—An abuse of confidence.—The new partner.—The compact.—The dead brought to life.—Saved from the wreck.—Legal advice.—Married for money.—A golden chance.—The intercepted letter.—A vision of wealth.—The forgery.—Within an inch of his life.—The rescue.—Tableau.

Act II. Scene as before; time, night.—Dark clouds gathering.—Changing the jackets.—Father and son.—On duty.—A struggle for fortune.—Loved for himself.—The divided greenbacks.—The agreement.—An unhappy life.—The detective's mistake.—Arrested.—Mistaken identity.—The likeness again.—On the right track.—The accident.—"Will she be saved?"—Latour's bravery.—A noble sacrifice.—The secret meeting.—Another case of mistaken identity.—The murder.—"Who did it?"—The torn cuff.—"There stands the murderer!"—"'Tis false!"—The wrong man murdered.—Who was the victim!—Tableau.

Act III. Two Days Later.—Plot and counterplot.—Gentleman and convict.—The price of her life.—Some new documents.—The divided banknotes.—Sunshine through the clouds.—Prepared for a watery grave.—Deadly peril.—Father and daughter.—The rising tide.—A life for a signature.—True unto death.—Saved.—The mystery solved.—Dénouement.—Tableau.

THE GYPSIES' FESTIVAL.

PRICE, 25 CENTS.

A Musical Entertainment for Young People. Introduces the Gypsy Queen, Fortune Teller, Yankee Peddler and a Chorus of Gypsies, of any desired number. The scene is supposed to be a Gypsy Camp. The costumes are very pretty, but simple; the dialogue bright; the music easy and tuneful; and the drill movements and calisthenics are graceful. Few properties and no set scenery required, so that the entertainment can be represented on any platform.

HELMER'S
ACTOR'S MAKE-UP BOOK.

A Practical and Systematic Guide to the Art of Making up for the Stage.

PRICE, 25 CENTS.

With exhaustive treatment on the Use of Theatrical Wigs and Beards, The Make-up and its requisite materials, the different features and their management, Typical Character Masks, etc. With Special Hints to Ladies. Designed for the use of Actors and Amateurs, and for both Ladies and Gentlemen. Copiously Illustrated.

CONTENTS.

I. Theatrical Wigs.—The Style and Form of Theatrical Wigs and Beards. The Color and Shading of Theatrical Wigs and Beards. Directions for Measuring the Head. To put on a Wig properly.

II. Theatrical Beards.—How to fashion a Beard out of crêpé hair. How to make Beards of Wool. The growth of Beard simulated.

III. The Make-up.—A successful Character Mask, and how to make it. Perspiration during performance, how removed.

IV. The Make-up Box.—Grease Paints. Grease paints in sticks; Flesh Cream; Face Powder; How to use face powder as a liquid cream; The various shades of face powder. Water Cosmétique. Nose Putty. Court Plaster. Cocoa Butter. Crêpé Hair and Prepared Wool. Grenadine. Dorin's Rouge. "Old Man's" Rouge. "Juvenile" Rouge. Spirit Gum. Email Noir. Bear's Grease. Eyebrow Pencils. Artist's Stomps. Powder Puffs. Hares' Feet. Camels'-hair Brushes.

V. The Features and their Treatment.—The Eyes: blindness. The Eyelids. The Eyebrows: How to paint out an eyebrow or moustache; How to paste on eyebrows; How to regulate bushy eyebrows. The Eyelashes: To alter the appearance of the eyes. The Ears. The Nose: A Roman nose; How to use the nose putty; A pug nose; An African nose; a large nose apparently reduced in size. The Mouth and Lips: a juvenile mouth; an old mouth; a sensuous mouth; a satirical mouth; a one-sided mouth; a merry mouth; A sullen mouth. The Teeth. The Neck, Arms, Hands and Fingernails: Fingernails lengthened. Wrinkles: Friendliness and Sullenness indicated by wrinkles. Shading. A Starving character. A Cut in the Face. A Thin Face Made Fleshy.

VI. Typical Character Masks.—The Make-up for Youth: Dimpled cheeks. Manhood. Middle Age. Making up as a Drunkard: One method; another method. Old Age. Negroes. Moors. Chinese. King Lear. Shylock. Macbeth. Richelieu. Statuary. Clowns.

VII. Special Hints to Ladies.—The Make-up. Theatrical Wigs and Hair Goods.

☞ In ordering, please specify **Helmer's** Make-up Book. ✍

THE ETHIOPIAN DRAMA.

PRICE 15 CENTS EACH.

THE AMATEUR AND VARIETY STAGE.

PRICE 15 CENTS EACH.

Any of the above will be sent by mail on receipt of the price, by

HAROLD ROORBACH, Publisher,

Successor to Roorbach & Company.

P. O. Box 3410.   9 Murray Street, New York.

A Drama in Five Acts, by H. V. Vogt.

Price, 15 Cents.

Nine male, three female characters, *viz.:* Leading and Second Juvenile Men, Old Man, Genteel Villain, Walking Gentleman, First and Second Light Comedians, Heavy Character, Low Comedian, Leading and Second Juvenile Ladies and Comic Old Maid. Time of playing, Two hours and a half.

SYNOPSIS OF EVENTS.

Act I. Love vs. Impulse.—Doller-clutch's office.—A fruitless journey, a heap of accumulated business and a chapter of unparalleled impudence.—News from the front.—A poor girl's trouble and a lawyer's big heart.—Hilda's sad story.—"I 'll see this thing through if it costs me a fortune!"—A sudden departure in search of a clue — The meeting of friends.—One of nature's noblemen.—Maitland betrays his secret by a slip of the tongue.—The ball at Beachwood.—Two spooneys, fresh from college, lose their heads and their hearts. —"Squashed, by Jupiter!'—Trusting innocence and polished villainy.—The interrupted tryst. — An honest man's avowal.—A picture of charming simplicity.—Murdell and Hilda meet face to face.—"I dare you to make another victim!"—A scoundrel's discomfiture.—Tableau.

Act II. The Separation.—The Maitland homestead.—Anastasia's doubts.—A warm welcome and its icy reception. —Forebodings and doubts.—Father and son.—Searching questions.—A domestic storm and a parent's command.—A foiled villain's wrath.—Enlisting for the war.—The collapse of the cowards.—" It 's no use, 'Dolphy, the jig 's up !"—Hilda's sympathy and Adrienne's silent despair.—The result of impulse.—The father pleads for his son.—Anastasia and Dollerclutch.—Coriolanus comes to grief.—Good and bad news.—Husband and wife.—Reginald demands an explanation.—A hand without a heart.—The separation.—A new recruit.—Too late; the roll is signed.—Tableau.

Act III. Duty vs. Impulse.—Four years later.—A camp in the army.—Longings. — "Only six miles from home!"—The skeleton in the closet.—A father's yearning for his child.—A woman-hater in love.—Dollerclutch's dream.—A picture of camp life and fun. —Coriolanus has his revenge.—News from home.—Dollerclutch makes a big find. "Eureka ! "—Proofs of Hilda's parentage and marriage.—A happy old lawyer.—"I 'll take them to Hilda !"—Detailed for duty.—A soldier's temptation.—The sentinel deserts his post.—The snake in the grass.—"At last, I can humble his pride !"

Act IV. The Reconciliation and Sequel.—At Reginald's home.—News from the army.—" Grant is not the man to acknowledge defeat!"—Adrienne and Hilda.—False pride is broken.—The reconciliation.—" Will Reginald forgive me ?"—Dollerclutch brings joy to Hilda's heart.—" You are the daughter of Morris Maitland !"—The stolen documents and the snake in the grass.—"Hang me if I don't see this thing through !"—A letter to the absent one.—Face to face.—The barrier of pride swept down.—"Reginald, I love you; come back !"—The happy reunion.—An ominous cloud.—" I have deserted my post ; the penalty is death. I must return ere my absence is discovered !"—The wolf in the sheepfold.—A wily tempter foiled. — A villain's rage. — "Those words have sealed your doom !" — The murder and the escape. — Dollerclutch arrives too late.—The pursuit.

Act V. Divine Impulse.—In camp.—Maitland on duty.—The charge of desertion and the examination.—"I knew not what I did !"—The colonel's lenity.—Disgrace.—News of Adrienne's murder is brought to camp.—Circumstantial evidence fastens the murder upon Reginald.—The court-martial.—Convicted and sentenced to be shot.—Preparations for the execution.—' God knows I am innocent! "—Dollerclutch arrives in the nick of time.—"If you shoot that man you commit murder !"—The beginning of the end.—" Adrienne lives!"—A villain's terror.—Adrienne appears on the scene.—" There is the attempted assassin !"—Divine impulse.—The reward of innocence and the punishment of villainy.—Good news.—" Hurrah, the war is over; Lee has surrendered to Grant!" —The happy *denouement* and *finale*.—Tableau.

Copies mailed, post-paid, to any address on receipt of the advertised price.

HAROLD ROORBACH, Publisher,
9 MURRAY ST., NEW YORK.

www.ingramcontent.com/pod-product-compliance
Lightning Source LLC
Chambersburg PA
CBHW021635270326
41931CB00008B/1040